Up and Away

Rita M Wood

Pen Press

First published in Great Britain by Pen Press

All paper used in the printing of this book has been made from wood
grown in managed, sustainable forests.

ISBN: 978-1-78003-553-6

Printed and bound in the UK
Pen Press is an imprint of
Indepenpress Publishing Limited
25 Eastern Place
Brighton
BN2 1GJ

A catalogue record of this book is available from
the British Library

Cover design by Jacqueline Abromeit

Preface

Why write a book on travelling? Many have been written!

All the holidays included have been taken somewhere out of England. Some have only been day tours, others have been for longer periods of time, particularly the one in 1996 to Singapore, Australia and New Zealand. All the day tours and the visits to Moscow and St Petersburg were taken through Palmair of Bournemouth. This company has been top of the world for flying, a family company. Unfortunately the owner has died and the company no longer survives.

After each tour, I have taken notes and now I feel it is time to make use of them.

Three friends and my husband accompanied me at various times. Rosemary and I were at school together in 1949 and the 50s. Jenny was one of my staff at work, but we have both retired and had similar interests. Dennis was a neighbour for several years but sadly died of cancer soon after the 1996 trip. Clive, my husband, has managed trips of late after retiring.

The following may give someone the incentive to travel and see how someone else lives; it also shows that it is possible to travel on your own and not be lonely.

Contents

Returning from Danmark
(four weeks)

Working in Danmark would make a book on its own as I was out there for one year before following on with the tour home in 1959! If I had come home on my own, tax would have been payable, so my sister came out and enjoyed the trip on my scooter, and I was repaid at home.

Just before leaving the country I received a letter from the customs officer in the nearby town, requesting my presence as the scooter was not taxed in Danmark. I attended on my own, having learnt 'some' of the language. The officer spoke but very little English, so fun was had with him trying to understand English; I knew he was trying to extract quite a lot of money from me, so of course I could not understand him! I had already written to the Automobile Association about my tax having run out on the scooter; they had suggested I pay as I ventured into other countries, so the Danish officer gave up and waved me out of his office!

My sister met me in Kobenhavn, so I took her around a little of Danmark and southern Sweden, visiting many places of interest I had been able to see. We visited an agriculture college in Sweden as we had been told that the Head could speak English, as I did not understand Swedish. One thing I have not forgotten: the cowshed had the walls painted blue to stop the flies coming into the building and annoying the cattle. From here we drove to the borders of Norway; my sister's time was limited, so we went no further into the country, but the smell of the pine forests was beautiful.

Sweden

Hojgaard (where author worked)

Back to where I worked in Lolland to collect some luggage and meet everyone to say goodbye, before starting the tour south. The ferry took us from Rodby to Lubeck in Germany; this was while the split of east and west existed. We saw signs to eastern Germany, 15 kilometres away. This was the nearest we wished to get to the barrier; the thought of being close gave us the creeps! We proceeded southwest to Hamburg but did not stay there long;

on to Bremen and to Groningen in the Netherlands, stopping at a small hotel overnight. Neither of us spoke German, so we chose to eat mushroom omelette every night while in Germany as we understood 'mushroom'. 'Coffee' and 'orange juice' we could also understand. The weather was very kind to us; we originally wrapped up well expecting the worst, but the further south we travelled the warmer it got. The end of April can still have cold spells.

At the Dutch border no one asked us about any tax or insurance for the scooter so we just kept driving. Two of us plus luggage on board and with flat land the petrol was lasting well with approximately 100 miles to the gallon!

At Arnhem we stopped to look round by the famous bridge from the Second World War; this was where many soldiers had died. You could still see the remains of bullet marks and where larger explosions had marked many buildings close by. Utrecht had more modern roads and had repairs completed quicker than Arnhem.

For two or three days we stayed on the outskirts of the Hague, having passed by many bulb fields. While at the hotel we learnt that a large display of bulbs was further down the coast at Keukenhof: 65 acres, and completely covered with bulbs of all colours and shapes. Separate patches were planted by different growers. We certainly arrived at the correct time to see the best of the blooms. Tulips were there in their hundreds and thousands, and other bulbs were in bloom. This was a photographer's heaven. A lake and stream and windmill added to the atmosphere, as did the girls in national costume. This is somewhere I will never forget.

The next stop was Rotterdam, where we drove through a long tunnel, not easy with the lights flashing by; when we arrived at the further end it appeared that the lights were still coming at us, leaving us with a horrible sensation. Breda was not far and then on to the outskirts of Antwerp, well known as being a busy city even in 1959. From the road cranes of various heights could be seen at the docks. The land was very flat and uninteresting so it was time to press on towards our French destination.

Keukenhof Gardens

The Belgian/French border came in sight and then the trouble started. We were pulled up at the border and the police started asking questions which I could not understand. My sister was left standing by the scooter while I was marched between two gendarmes to the office to someone with more control. After a few minutes it was found he could not speak English; after some sign language, he waved his hands in disgust. I knew he was trying to extract some money for the scooter. Eventually I was marched back and told to go. Just as I started up the scooter a car arrived from France; the driver was asked if he could speak English, and ended up translating. He said that we had to pay a considerable number of francs in tax, as the scooter did not have a tax disk. Such is life!

After the travelling and all the excitement it was time to find a hotel in Bethune. The only one available and suitable was adjoining the main railway with the windows looking out onto the track! Although tired, we had little sleep. The following day was spent looking round the town and the thousands of war graves, both for 1914–18 and for 1939–45. I suppose we took more notice of the cemeteries as Madame Birch's husband looked after the English graves. During the war, because Mr Birch was English, he and his family were over in England as refugees. Madame Birch worked for our father on the farm while Mr Birch went gardening for a large house close by. They returned to France after the war.

Arras was a town on our route that had also had been in the war zone. By the time we reached Cambrai the temperature was rising, so we had to start shedding some of our clothes and packing them in a bag on the back of the scooter. Cambrai was on a hill; drainage from the houses at the side of the road was running down the gutter to the bottom of the hill, only to end up in a pond with ducks.

Saint-Quentin was the area we were aiming for as Savy par Entrier was not far from there. We lost the actual direction we should have travelled, so we stopped at a house to ask. It so happened they were English-speaking, and we were invited in and given a glass of their homemade raspberry wine; they knew Madame Birch, so they got their car out and led us to her house. It was strange to happen across someone who actually knew the person we were to meet; in fact they were good friends.

The greeting with Madame Birch was very warm, especially as we had not seen her since she had left in 1946. It was not known how long we would stay as, if you went to the back door of her house in England, it was not unusual to see chickens fly out of the kitchen and into the garden. Cleanliness was one of our concerns! She had been very insistent that we visit her in France, in her home.

When Mr and Madame Birch returned to France, they told us only the walls were standing, no roof and no windows. This must have been heartbreaking and such hard work had to be put into getting the house back into living conditions. The house was built in stone and contained two bedrooms and a kitchen-cum-living room. The toilet was at the bottom of the garden and presumably the tin bath hanging outside on the wall was brought in for washing or bathing. Unfortunately Mr Birch had died a year before we arrived. Madame was left to make her own living with three acres of ground, some calves and a cow. In the garden she reared her own chickens, selling chicken, eggs and vegetables in the local market. She drove an old rickety van to carry produce to the market. She must have been about 65 by now so it was hard work making sufficient money to live.

She told us she made coffee once a week, and by the time we arrived it was several days old and had been heated every day; it was somewhat like syrup, very thick and stronger by the day! It did not help that my sister did not like coffee! It got to the stage when neither of us could cope with it. Madame left us in the kitchen with the breakfast while she went down the garden to feed her chickens. We poured the coffee down the sink only to find the drain ran onto the path to the chickens; it was amazing how much two cups looked like when running down a dry path!

The day came for us to move on. Having heard so much about the beaches and Dunkirk we felt it necessary to stop and see them. The beaches were far bigger than I had imagined and when the tide went out there was just a thin blue line on the horizon. Some time was spent on the beach and sand dunes thinking about the horrors of war the forces endured. We visited Calais airport as we planned to fly back to England from there. The passage was booked with a place for the scooter, then we spent time sitting on the hill at the entrance to the harbour of Calais. There were still large gun holes which the Germans had made, probably protecting all sizes of boats going in and out, as well as forces attacking the English and French during the war.

The following morning it was back to the airport ready to return to England. Everything went smoothly, and we took to the air. It was a small aircraft and as we rose into the air it was possible to see the white cliffs of Dover. We were the only two passengers and the scooter the only vehicle.

On our landing at Lydd airport in Kent, the Automobile Association met us and so we just walked through customs, even with half a Danish tea service in the luggage!

Looking back on this trip, it would have been better to have had more time to make more of each stop, to visit museums and more places of interest, but even so my sister paid her financial share so I had some money until I found work.

Italy
November 1972
(long weekend)

Four of us from work decided to go to Italy for a long weekend in November. We stayed in a hotel in Sorrento which was pre-booked for us. Owing to fog and bad weather in Italy we were delayed and our Naples landing was cancelled. The aircraft landed at a small airport outside Rome; en route we had a beautiful view of Mont Blanc, but were disappointed as my camera was in the luggage. Ever since, when travelling, the camera has always been with me. While we circled over the City of Rome, there was a marvellous view of the Vatican and St Peter's Square.

Our coaches were waiting for us at Naples and had not received the message until we had landed, so we had to wait until they came to Rome, which was some distance; in fact it took them nearly two hours to arrive. It was then a three-hour trip down to Sorrento. We eventually arrived at 10pm; the hotel had saved a meal for us but when served it was almost cold. Everyone was tired and just to help I developed a migraine! During the dinner we were asked if we would like to go to Capri the next day. I declined as I felt so tired.

Our rooms were very pleasant. Mine overlooked the mountain with lemon and orange trees growing on the side; I could almost touch them. In the morning one of the cooks came and picked the fresh lemons which were turned into a gorgeous sorbet for the evening meal. The floor was a warm marble over most of the hotel.

Our group joined together for breakfast and found none of us were going to the isle of Capri. Later in the day we were told that we did not miss much. Gracie Fields was living on the island, but apparently lived much like a recluse and few people ever saw her. The Blue Grotto was included in the boat trip.

As for us, courtesy of the milk marketing board, we had an enjoyable walk round Sorrento, visiting some of the small back streets, where I purchased a beautiful leather handbag which was used for many years after. The volcano Vesuvius could be seen from the town. In the early morning it looked very mysterious with the peak showing and the remainder shrouded in mist. One could just see the movement of the sea below in the bay. The actual beach was very dirty with a considerable amount of flotsam around, on land and in the water. When one looked back at Sorrento from the wooden pier, the sheerness of the cliffs was striking; they just dropped straight into the water. Buildings built on top were on the very edge. It would have been possible to open a window and abseil straight down to the beach. The main roads in town meandered up and down hills. There were few cars, mostly horse-drawn vehicles; this gave an impression of stepping back in time.

The following day we were taken on a tour of Naples and Pompeii, which was worthwhile, particularly the stop at Pompeii. I shall always remember this place. One hears so much about it, so seeing it first-hand was essential: the remains of the buildings and people who had started to run from the lava and yet been caught when falling, where they tried to get away. There was even a burnt loaf of bread retrieved from an oven that had been cooking at the time. I would have loved to spend more time than we had to study things further, it was so interesting.

Not far from here was the famous cameo factory where jewellery was hand-carved from shells that had been gathered from the local bay. The shells had two different layers of colour, so the top was removed while carving designs through to the second layer. Many were set in gold as broaches, pendants and rings. I remember in the car park outside the factory a wall was covered with bougainvillea, a completely covered wall.

We were driven up the road on the lower part of the volcano Vesuvius in a car. The road twisted and turned with hairpin bends until we ran out of road. It was then we had to walk the remainder of the way to the top. As we got nearer the top we could feel our shoes getting hotter and hotter underneath. As we neared the pinnacle a guide was waiting and he explained about the crater and that the last eruption had been in 1946; it normally went up every 25 years. We looked 50 or 60 feet into the centre; several places along the sides were smoking with large patches of sulphur around. The lava flows from the last eruption were very visible as they were still barren, no greenery or flowers. These flows remain barren for many years as it takes so long for them to cool down.

In Italy vehicles drive on the right of the road and our car was so close to sheer drops into the sea, going through tunnels and round sharp bends, when returning to Sorrento.

This was an interesting tour to remember, especially when other volcanos come alive and cause devastation in various parts of the world.

Pompeii

View of the Bay of Sorrento

Hong Kong, China and Thailand
March 1986
(three weeks)

Rosemary, my school friend, decided to go out east to see part of Asia and asked me to join her, as she did not want to travel on her own. This was the first long-haul flight and holiday I had taken and it was 15 hours' journey. We flew over Munich and the Gulf of Bahrain and on to Bombay for refuelling. When we landed at the airport there were shacks with galvanised roofs all round the perimeter; the places looked like pigsties, but humans lived in them. We left the aircraft while it refuelled. I found a craft shop while waiting. Many filigree pendants and bracelets were on show so I could not resist purchasing one. There was much imitation ivory, and at a price.

The temperature was 22°C with very hazy sunshine; it was daylight, 9am in Bombay and 2am English time. We loaded and started to move back towards the runway, but had to return to the bay as there were problems with the fuel valve, which had to be replaced; this meant a replacement had to be flown in from somewhere else. Everything was switched off, so no air conditioning. We finally left three hours later when everyone was sweltering in the heat.

Breakfast was served after we had taken off; lovely fresh fruit was on the menu after a mushroom omelette and coffee. Some films were shown during the flight. As it was quiet it was time to try and sleep. The flight took four and three-quarter hours before arriving at Hong Kong.

To land at Hong Kong we had to fly between tall buildings. This was the normal flight path; I understand this was the most difficult airport to land an aircraft. Since those days a new airport has been built and it is now easier to land. The word Hong Kong means 'Scented Bay', so called because Aberdeen (on the island) made perfumed sticks. We had booked a hotel on the island, where we were taken by courtesy car.

The following day, a Sunday, we met friends of Rosemary's who were living there. They took us to the famous Stanley Market and although it was March, only a cardigan was required. The Market was a fascinating place, a must for all tourists, where all types of goods and souvenirs were for sale, all at reasonable prices compared to the main town shops.

From here we walked down to the beach where a Shinto temple is on the promenade. It is dedicated to the goddess of the sea. There are two figures that stand as tall as the first floor of a building. On the way back Rosemary's friend Alistair took us round the other side of Hong Kong Island, so now we had been all the way round.

The following day we were driven through the tunnel to Kowloon and on to Clear Water Bay where Alistair and his wife Jean lived. They had a beautiful house way above what they would have been able to afford in England. Also they had a maid to do the housework. Alistair worked as a pilot for Cathay Pacific airlines. The house was rented at £112 per month. Papaya trees, hibiscus and lantana were growing like weeds in both the garden and surrounding rough ground. They provided the evening meal for us consisting of carrots, bamboo shoots, celery and minced meat pancakes. After the meal we visited the famous Star Ferry when we crossed back to the island and finally we took a taxi to the Midnight Market or so-called 'poor man's nightclub'. We stopped to explore the market as it was brightly lit up. This was followed by a tram ride back to the hotel. We actually passed the stop where we should have left the tram, so after alighting we stopped and asked a policeman for directions. He stopped a taxi for us and eventually we arrived back at the hotel. By this time it was pouring with rain so we had a dash into the hotel!

The next day Rosemary wished to see more friends at the University of Hong Kong. I wanted to visit China so I left her for the day and we went our separate ways. I was met at our hotel by a courier and taken by taxi to the hydrofoil, then it crossed to

Macau. There was a swell on the sea, which gave us a swinging ride, and I remember passing many islands and fishing boats. The boats had bamboo rods about 20 foot long on either side of the vessels. Each rod had fishing nets trawling in the sea.

Our journey took one and a quarter hours, and on arrival a coach awaited us. When travelling it had all the squeaks and shakes possible, but we made it through Macau and then to the Chinese border. Macau was a very poor area, and under Portuguese rule. At the border we all had to dismount from the coach and follow our leader who was waving a flag for us to follow.

We were each given a number and we had to stand in numerical order, one behind the other. If we moved out of line the armed guards moved us back into position. On looking back it now seems amusing, but not at the time. It was a very abrupt way of treating tourists! It took a considerable amount of time to get the whole coach load through customs. The coach had been sealed before crossing the border to wait for us.

A Chinese guide who could speak good English came on the coach after we had gone through customs. He produced a great deal of propaganda praising communism, this obviously being the main reason for acting as a guide. The coach stopped only at places which the communists wished us to see, then we could photograph places such as the paddy fields. The women were busy planting the rice in the wet fields. Water buffalo were turning the soil over, ploughing the sides of the fields.

One place we were taken was a village commune. The poverty was unbelievable; many houses had earthen floors. An old lady was doubled up with arthritis; her house had a straw roof and sides, no glass in the windows. It was like stepping back in time! At the entrance to all houses, we were told, was a high step which made people bow to enter: a sign of respect, as an effigy of their god was placed opposite the entrance. One house we visited had three rooms for three generations; the walls were solid, probably cement. Furniture was sparse: a sideboard which also contained a television set; a small table the size of our card table and two chairs; nothing else. The second room contained a bed – the remainder of the family slept on mattresses on the floor – and the third room at the back contained a sink and an ancient cooker.

When the children were young the grandparents were expected to look after them so that mother and father could work out in the paddy fields.

Another place visited was the local school; there were concrete floors, windows with no glass and some tables for the children to work at. As winters are cold, one could only imagine how the children would be wrapped up in coats and scarves! The local shop had so little inside, hardly any goods available. Not really enough to be called a shop!

We next stopped at a resort that had hot springs and a hotel. There we had lunch; I sat with a Japanese family who spoke perfect English. The food was pleasant to taste and there was a variety from which to choose. The ladies' loos had doors like the western type seen in films, at least 18 inches from the floor, and only as high as your shoulders! We had a laugh! Opposite the hotel was the equivalent of a supermarket, and not knowing the language, we had no idea of the prices. Next door was a souvenir shop, which also had prices which we could understand. Some were worth looking at and were a reasonable price, jewellery, pots and pictures being the predominant articles for sale.

After a short journey we were taken to a house where Doctor Sun Yat-sen had been born. He was responsible for the overthrow of the last dynasty and instigated communism in China. His house had been made into a museum and tourists were welcomed. After this there was approximately an hour's journey back to the borders where we went through the same regimentation to leave the country, and then on to Macau and finally on the hydrofoil back to Hong Kong Island. A very interesting day out!

Rosemary and I met up with her friends, then crossed on the Star Ferry to Kowloon for an evening meal. The Star Ferry carries pigs and chickens on the lower floor while ordinary passengers travel on the upper deck; quite an unusual ferry. Fish was always on the menus, wherever you went, and I do not care for fish, other than fried fish or boiled prawns; there was not a large choice for me! Afterwards we stopped and viewed the lights on the island; everywhere was lit up with signs, coloured lights and adverts. This as usual gave us another late night! We had actually made the most of the time while here.

The following day we decided to look round the streets close by, which nearly all contained shops of some description. Hong Kong smelt strongly of boiled fish, spice and coriander, no matter where we went. When tiring of shopping we went to see the Tiger Balm Gardens, a must for tourists. A Chinese man originally designed them in 1935; he adored things of beauty. It is very difficult to explain how the rocks had been carved, showing exotic pictures of birds and dragons.

Wall decorations in Tiger Balm Gardens

The house was lavishly built with a large pagoda roof, but from one extreme to another: behind the house there was the steep side of a mountain, and there sheds and shacks had been built. In England even chickens would have better places to sleep! We learnt that these were homes of Chinese immigrants, built of bits and pieces of wood and galvanised sheeting which had been salvaged from the bottom of the hill. When Hong Kong had heavy rain all these places were washed away from the mountain and the immigrants had to rebuild their homes, carrying what they could find at the bottom of the mountain.

From here we visited Victoria Peak. A rail coach travelled to the top, but we were in the cloud and so could see nothing of the view. Returning to the bottom we paid a visit to the 'ladder streets' of Aberdeen; these were so called as they were up or down steps in side streets on the side of Victoria Peak. These had market stalls selling gifts, clothes, fruit and vegetables.

Tuk-tuk, a method of transport

There was a restaurant at the quay in Aberdeen called the 'Jumbo Floating Restaurant'; a rowing boat took you across to it. There was exotic decor inside, both at the entrance and on a second floor. We had a very pleasant fish meal! There was entertainment for the patrons of the evening, some telling mystical tales, and the actors were in beautiful coloured costumes all with large headdresses. This was certainly an evening with a difference.

Next morning some general shopping not far from our hotel, and prices were very reasonable. This was our last chance before leaving for the airport later in the day. The overall impression of Hong Kong was that it was very interesting but the standard of living was split, average and very poor! The place will always be remembered by the smell. We did not feel under threat of being mugged, everyone was very polite and courteous, and overall it was somewhere to return to.

The next country on our tour was Thailand, and so we had two and a half hours' flight, including a meal, to Bangkok. The airport was several kilometres from the city; the atmosphere was very hot and humid. It was evening when we arrived and in contrast to Hong Kong there were very few lights to be seen. A guide met us and escorted us to the hotel bus. It seemed very strange as we could see our hotel across the dual carriageway but there were no means of crossing; you had to go down to Bangkok and cross over the road to the other side of the dual carriageway and return!

The following morning the guide came to the hotel to meet us, and just the two of us plus guide were taken in a car to two temples. The first held the Golden Buddha, and like all people going inside we removed our shoes in respect. This Buddha weighed five and a half English tons and was only about five foot high. The second temple contained the 'Reclining Buddha'; this was 150 feet long and 40 feet high. This one was covered in gold leaf which was unfortunately peeling, but like many things it would take time and money to restore. Little altars were set up in several places round the Buddha with flowers, incense and gold leaf placed there by the public. Many monks were in these temples; it takes three years to be a monk, their heads are shaven and they wear orange sari robes. As in Nepal, most men in Thailand spend a certain time in their life as a monk.

As we found later, on these tours the guides take their clients at every possible moment to jewellery factories. After this first tour I bought several pieces as the price was very reasonable, especially after bartering. I chose an emerald ring; as it was too small they would enlarge it and deliver it to the hotel at no extra cost. When I eventually received it I was sure it was not the original as it was a different design; being in a foreign country, I felt I had to be careful what I said.

We returned to the hotel having purchased some food from a supermarket, sat and ate it in the shade, in the garden. We suddenly realised that we should be at the airport to fly to the north! We scrambled to put everything together and dashed. On arrival it was found our seats had been taken so we were upgraded at no extra cost. We received another free meal on board, with the flight taking one hour.

We flew from Bangkok up to Chiang Mai; I had a streaming cold and flying made it worse.

At Chiang Mai we had another courier meet us at the airport with a car just for us! The gentleman was not quite so good with his English, but we got used to him. Both driver and guide were part Chinese and part Thai. We arrived at our lodgings in time to catch up on sleep with an early night. The hotel there was very pleasant, with balconies so we had a little fresh air. Our meal was an enormous fresh fruit salad which produced at least half a glass of juice, gorgeous!

It was Good Friday at home, but just a normal working day in Thailand. The breakfast was served on the terrace at the hotel, with scrambled egg, toast, croissants, pineapple jam, orange juice and coffee. The trees in the grounds were in flower and had a strong perfume, with plenty of dust blowing in the wind; it felt as though a period of cold was beginning.

Thailand is famous for its lacquered ornaments so we went to a factory to see how they were made. One thing was strange: there were no walls, only a roof to the factory. This was owing to the high temperature and humidity, which could be as high as 27°C. The design allowed air to circulate through the place; I could not call it a building. The goods were made from bamboo, coated with gum. This came from a special tree which was grown within the locality. Twelve coats of the gum were applied, and allowed to dry between each application; this took between four and five days. Then the artistic part was carried out; each article was very delicately painted with different designs. The workers sat on wooden benches (no cushions) and crossed legs while working.

Silk was used in most cloth and clothes so once again we had to see how the silk was made. First we were greeted with a drink of cola, as we had also been at the previous place. With the humidity we perspired so much that we needed to replace the liquid. There was a demonstration showing us how the silk was collected, spun and dyed before being woven into material for garments. They were expensive to buy; a dress cost the equivalent of £40 or £50. The colours were really beautiful, but we came away without any purchases!

On the itinerary was a stop at a teak factory where the carving of wood took place. In some respects it was like other factories we had seen; no walls, the men sitting on wooden benches, crossed legs, but this time working with chisels between their crossed legs. This looked very dangerous; what happens if the chisel slips? We noticed that the people were very slim! A few workers had drawn the design on the wood; others just chipped away having decided the design in their mind. Apparently if the father is very good, the son is automatically taken on and trained to do the same type of carving. Like father, like son!

Like all factories one was expected to purchase something, but everything on offer seemed so expensive. The umbrella factory was almost as bad, but various skills were demonstrated, ending with the most beautiful paintings done without any help of a sketch! The painters used very bold strokes with the paintbrush.

We returned to the hotel for lunch, and boiled some water for safety as we had heard of tourists picking up local bugs from the water. The local people had become immune to most. It got dark early by 6.30pm; the hotel had its own generator, but candles and matches were provided for each room as the generator often gave up. The previous night we were only lit by candle on two occasions when the generator broke down; apparently this was a common occurrence.

The hotel bus took us down to the city of Chiang Mai for the night market; it was great fun bartering for goods. I bought a length of material for the equivalent of £1 and have since made a full-length evening skirt. It was fascinating seeing some of the tribal embroidery that the nomadic tribes had brought in to sell.

We hired a tuk-tuk to take us back to the hotel. These are three-wheeled and small, with a two-stroke engine: just a small vehicle which two passengers and the driver can squeeze into! There are no sides, but just a canvas roof. This method of travelling is much cheaper than hiring a taxi. The tuk-tuk was lovely and cool although the temperature was almost 27°C; by now we were getting acclimatised to the higher temperatures.

After a really good night's sleep, it was breakfast and then a trip to the orchid farm with our guide. The climate was suitable for breeding and growing the flowers of many colours and types. Most were grown on the trees or in special pots. The nursery was trying to grow different colours and shapes.

The next journey was up in the hills to a nomadic tribe, mostly on unmade roads. The soil was very red, and in places the rain had washed away the sides of the road. The scenery was mostly scrub with some wooded areas, but not as heavily wooded as in England. Many small hills had a haze hanging over them owing to the humidity.

We eventually arrived at the Mao village. All the housing was homemade shacks, thatched with reeds, and plain earth floors. Many people were only partially clothed, both children and adults the same. An elderly man offered to smoke a pipe of opium if we paid him. Through our guide we had it translated that we did not believe in smoking drugs. Children and women alike came to us trying to sell some of their embroidered articles. In the village they kept some black pigs, which were a local breed. They were kept in an open shack which was thatched. A Brahmin cow was tethered round the neck, under a tree. We found it amazing that the residents were of mixed blood, namely Chinese, Thai and Burmese, and lived like nomads in the hills.

Nearer Chiang Mai we went to see the elephants. When we arrived they were being bathed in the river and thoroughly enjoying it. Even the babies had a dip! Later some gave a demonstration of how they worked in the forests logging. One animal not working was tethered by the foot and members of the public were able to go and handle the creature, if they were brave enough! Rosemary laughed as I went up to the animal and talked to it; she thought it funny as it would not understand English. Personally I do not think it matters as they understand if you like animals! I felt the skin on its side and down the trunk; it was very rough! The baby elephant was small but very strong, and lovely at only a few months old. We sat under a shelter to watch the demonstration of how the mature animals work. While we watched, a cheeky gibbon came and took a banana from one of the tourists, much to our amusement. It soon disappeared up a tree and ate it!

Rosemary wished to see the University of Chiang Mai so our guide took us round the grounds. A beautiful large lake was situated within the campus. The university covered over 50 acres so it was very spacious for the students. Temperature was still rising so we returned to the hotel to take life easy and discuss the morning's events.

At 7pm we were collected and taken to a traditional Thai dinner and dancing, which was held in the town. Once again we removed our shoes before entering. Our food table had been reserved for us and we sat on the floor propped up with cushions, but these kept slipping along the floor! The tables were brought to us covered in food, all in different bowls. The tables were only about 14 inches high. Rice was served in a woven basket and other food in china bowls. The meal started with a clear soup; it looked like water with two or three strips of chicken and a piece of celery, then followed fried chicken joints, curried beef, a tomato mixture with spices, banana fried in a super crisp batter, and coffee to drink served with a crispy rice biscuit.

When the meal was almost over the Thai dancing commenced. First eight women moved in formation at a very slow pace. A man then danced with 12 knives, showing his skills. One female carried lights on her hands; with the main lights turned off, this was very effective. The music to me had no real tune, but this was Thai music. At the end of the session we collected our shoes and went to the culture gardens, where we sat under electric fans as the temperature was still over 27°C. Here more dancing took place in local costume, accompanied by old instruments, one like an original reed accordion. Eventually it was time to return to the hotel for the night.

While looking at some leaflets and local maps I noticed there was a German/Thai farm close by. The hotel kindly telephoned them and found it was possible for me to make a visit. The following day I took a tuk-tuk and arrived at the farm manager's house. He was a little reserved at first, probably wondering what a female was doing being interested in a farm. He spoke very good English. This farm was the largest in North Thailand. There were 37 cows in milk, and 40 in-calf heifers. These were all tied up in the cowshed with only a roof overhead, no walls! They had a collar round the neck with a chain fixed above on a pole and the pole's other end fixed in the ground. This chain was threaded through a link on the collar.

The cows were a local breed crossed with Brahmin and crossed yet again with the American Friesian. The majority of the animals were a second cross, and were being crossed again with the Friesians. They were trying to get a larger cow. The local breed often did not supply sufficient milk to rear their own calf. The average milk yield for the herd was only 2000 kg, 4.1% fat and 3.26% protein. They were milked with Alfa Laval bucket machines. The cows were kept under this roof and fed mostly on rice straw which was very coarse, along with some hay and soya concentrates. This was distributed according to the production of the milk. A second farm was used for growing soya and hay; these were harvested in October after the rainy season.

The young calves were housed on slats; they apparently thrived better on wood. After they were weaned they went on to concrete floors. An experiment was being carried out: rearing the calves on soya milk, instead of cow's milk. The bull calves were sold for meat. The milk was sold in Chiang Mai for pasteurising and then sold in cartons for retail for approximately £1.23 per litre. The farm was connected to the university although students did no manual work on the farm. A very interesting morning!

In the afternoon we returned to the airport and thence to Bangkok. The following morning we found a shopping plaza to wander round; it was cooler inside; the humidity made the temperature 32°C. The museum in the famous Jim Thompson house was only a short walk away; he had done so much for the Thai silk industry. He disappeared on a trip to Malaysia, so his home was made a trust and opened to the public. All the money raised from this goes to the blind of Bangkok.

At our hotel the swimming pool was on the twelfth floor; it was amazing to me that the building was so high, with the swimming pool. By evening it was cooler but the smell of the drains had not altered!

A visit to the Royal Palace was on the itinerary, but not much was seen. At the temple of the Emerald Buddha special prayers were being said so no entry was allowed. Many people were sitting under 'shelters' outside the temple, their shoes removed, praying as the leader's voice was relayed over a microphone; there was a smell of burning incense.

Most of the tours started early to miss the afternoon heat, as did the following day's tour. We joined the two English couples at 6.45am, travelling in a minibus. It was amusing as one couple tried to outdo the other, with bigger and better properties and swimming pools at home etc. Rosemary and I sat in front having difficulty trying not to laugh!

We stopped en route to buy some coconut milk, but I did not enjoy it. On the sides of the road stalls were selling pomelos, a fruit much like a grapefruit, and people planting rice in paddy fields.

One of the main cemeteries visited was at Kanchanaburi, where many people were buried as a consequence of the Burma Railway's construction. So many people either died or were killed. We walked round the cemetery with many others, only they were looking for names on the headstones. A book at the entrance gave the name and the plot, then it was easier to find the grave. It was beautifully looked after with tradescantia planted at each grave. Each headstone was the same shape and colour, with name, regiment and age.

After this stop we were taken on to the River Kwai and a 'long-tailed' boat was hired for us. The boats were very narrow and it was only possible to sit one in front of the other; the 'tail' was four or five foot long and had the engine propeller at the back. This took us to an area in the jungle where the hospital had been situated at Chungkai. The only thing left were more and more graves, similar to the first ones we had visited. A Thai man was gardening there and I spoke to him. He said it was something he had to do in memory of all those who had died, or been killed by the Japanese. When he was a boy he threw bananas over the perimeter fence to the prisoners as they were starving. He was beaten several times by the Japanese when caught throwing the fruit over the fence. It seemed ironic; as we were talking in the cemetery a steam train rumbled and whistled in the distance, here where many had been forced to work on the Burma Railway.

On returning to the boat, we saw some people moving their home from one bank to the other. The house was floated across the river as it was made of wood, with various types of cane-like wood woven into the sides to make the walls. What was amazing was that the home was much like a house from the past, but it had a TV aerial, so they had either electricity or a battery. Children and parents alike were swimming and guiding the house to the opposite side of the river.

When we landed we were close to the actual 'Bridge over the River Kwai', where we walked for several minutes before we came back and walked over some floating planks to a restaurant. The planks overlapped one another, but it was rather perilous as they were narrow and tipped from one side to the other. The lunch consisted of a delicious clear soup, rice, sweet and sour fried chicken, an omelette, fresh watermelon and pineapple.

After all this it was time to return to the centre of Bangkok, and yet another jewellery factory. We complained, as this was not on our schedule; the guide was obviously paid to bring as many people to the factory as possible to make some commission. With a lot of persuasion the guide eventually got a taxi for us and we went back to the hotel. We were feeling a little cross, so on returning to the hotel we complained to the agents.

The next tour was of the canals of Bangkok, which included a trip to the royal barges. Five of us sailed from the quay at the Orient hotel; the other passengers were from New Zealand. The first stop was at the Cambodian Temple, called the 'Temple of Dawn'. A street market was at the quay where we landed; the Thai certainly make the most of their tourist spots. I climbed to the top of the temple; the steps were steep and we were almost standing on the heads of the people below!

The guide decided it was time to return to the quay where we had come from without seeing the barges. Once again we complained as the visit was on this tour and we had paid for it. He got off the boat, disappearing for a minute, and returned with a long face, saying that he had telephoned his employer and would have to hire another boat. We believed he was going to pocket the money for himself!

Eventually we did go and see the royal barges; they were very ornate with masses of gold decorations. They were only used for special occasions. Many oarsmen were required to paddle the barges.

When arriving back at the Orient hotel, we told the guide we would find our own way back to our hotel. At this time the Orient hotel was number one in the world. Earl Spencer and Princess Diana's mother were staying at the time. We walked through the foyer, which had the most gorgeous orchids and bamboo plants on display. White marble was everywhere; there were some shops but with very expensive goods. While there we had coffee on the patio, and much to our surprise it cost less than in our hotel! Later in the day, after returning to base we watched television and took life easy, as next morning we would have to be out by 7am.

This time it was a drive in a minibus; a stop was made to photograph a water buffalo. They are covered with very little hair, but have a very thick black skin; one had enormous horns, approximately four feet in length. We passed banana plantations, growing two varieties; one had short dumpy fruit and the other was like the ones we normally have at home. We also learnt there were two types of coconut; sugar was made from one variety. The Thai cut the new shoots, drained them, and then boiled until the water had evaporated. This left a brown sediment, which was sugar; this was then refined. We were given an invitation to visit this process, then to look inside the home of the workers. There were many cupboards all around the room but little other furniture. There was one bed and the other members of the family slept on mattresses placed on the floor. The coldest temperature they had was 11°C; they did not want to work then, but would rather stay in bed! There are three main seasons: wet July to October, cold November to March and sunny April to the wet season.

We stopped at some salt flats which were approximately an acre each in size. These were flooded with seawater, pumped from channels by windmills. It took about two weeks for the water to evaporate, after which groups of workers came and scraped the salt off the soil and stacked it in lumps to dry. Some salt was sold in bags along the side of the road. A Thai man was standing on a narrow path to the flats with a python; as people passed by he tried to get them to drape it round their necks. I refused to go near as I have a phobia of snakes! Later in the day I was walking in a crowd when a child came up to me with one and tried to pass it on to me. I quickly dodged to one side with my heart in my mouth!

The floating market which people abroad hear about was very interesting; only women sell their goods from the boats, while the men work in the fields to produce the fruit and vegetables. We bought 18 bananas for the equivalent of five pence – five pence! – and a large pineapple for 20 pence, and consequently lived on the two fruit for several days. In the souvenir shops we bartered and acquired some cheap gifts to take home. It was some time before our guide was able to get us together and on to a coach to the Rose Garden. I remember getting off the coach beside a lake that had trees hanging over the water with gorgeous yellow orchids hanging from the branches.

Lunch was taken in a floating building, no walls but a thatched roof; it was very cool. We met a couple from Cardiff who joined us on our table; this was embarrassing as the whole time the wife was telling her husband what he liked or disliked. Even he looked uncomfortable! We parted company at the end of the meal.

Special entertainment was laid on in the theatre for our benefit; this time the seats were raised like an English theatre, but with a bamboo roof. The costumes were very colourful; the cast showed some of the Thai customs and dances; the music was not very tuneful as we know our harmony. The gardens were spectacular round the theatre and consisted of nearly 50 acres. The orchids were growing everywhere, including in the trees. There were some elephants on show; I believe they had been giving rides to tourists. After all the excitement of the day we returned again to the hotel.

Pattaya was the next stop the following day; this was some 90 kilometres south, and we had yet another early start. A minibus collected us and took us to a main coach station, which we left in a beautiful modern coach with air conditioning, arriving at the new destination two and a half hours later. There were several traffic problems en route, which slowed the journey down. The resort was among hills; the coach had dropped some passengers in the town at hotels, and we were the last to leave. Our hotel was on the outskirts in a lovely quiet spot with our own beach. Later we were told that this hotel was the best in the area.

The view from our window looked out on a very large Buddha standing on the top of a hill. The view close at hand was over to a golf course, tennis courts, some scrub farmland and three different varieties of palm trees. The hotel had numerous restaurants; the first night we visited the seafood one. I had fried prawns in batter; these were the size of our hands; the warm seas made them grow much bigger than at home. The meal was completed with a banana split with three types of ice cream.

The sea was so warm, I sat on a groyne and enjoyed being half-submerged in the water. I had never been in such a warm sea before. A group of people were parascending, and several had water scooters. We were advised not to use a water scooter as a favourite trick on the part of those hiring them out was to say something was wrong with it when it was returned, when in fact it had not been perfect when hired!

A storm came up with sheet and fork lightning; it also poured with rain. This lasted for some time. Staff had to return to work, so took their shoes off and paddled through, holding an umbrella. The car park was flooded in no time. The temperature dropped but left the air humid.

For the evening meal we visited another restaurant and had a whole chargrilled lobster each, with salad and mooli, I had not tasted anything like it, and it was very cheap. This was followed with baked Alaska, super! The thought of the taste makes my mouth water! We were interested in buying snacks for lunch, as we had found them cheaper than hotel meals. Breakfast was included in the price but the remainder of meals we had to purchase. One evening we had beef stroganoff and finished with half a pineapple with mixed tropical fruit, really too large a serving.

So far we had avoided sunburn and had a slight tan; we kept out of the main heat during the day. There were other nationalities staying at our hotel but they kept to themselves.

One night we had gone to bed, but were sitting up and talking, when a lizard appeared on the wall opposite. It was about 12 inches long and had appeared through the air conditioning. We knew that they were harmless, so it was lights out and we turned over. No sign of it in the morning, but we did mention it to the staff on our landing. When we returned to the room in the evening, on each of our pillows was a beautiful orchid. Outside in the evenings there were always geckos, nearly white and up to three inches long; they could always be found around the top of the door or window frames. During the day they were on the ground; I had to be careful where I walked. They made a perpetual clicking sound.

One trip we made was to the coral island which we had seen from our beach. A boat was waiting for us on the town beach and it took us to Koh Larn. The sand there was pure white but sharp to bare feet, as it was coral. We were transferred to a glass-bottom boat but little was seen. I am not a good sea traveller, and felt sick on the way! When we landed I sat under an umbrella all day. Rosemary went to a cafe and enjoyed a fish meal; I just sat and watched water skis, scooters and people swimming. There were people walking up and down the beach trying to sell souvenirs.

To travel back we were expected to be agile as we had to paddle up to our knees to join the boat to return to Pattaya. The sea was shallow, so the boat could not get closer to the land. One man missed the boat and was brought out by scooter! The portly man was about to board when the scooter capsized. I wanted to laugh as the plump man had sunglasses and a straw hat with a brim; he shot into the sea and went under, leaving his hat to float. He was rescued by a long-tail boat, which hauled him aboard our boat; our passengers roared with laughter.

The crossing only took 45 minutes and the sea was perfectly smooth. By the time we reached land the man who had been 'dunked' had dried out. It seemed strange that while in Thailand we never thought of taking a cardigan or coat with us; it was always so warm. The coldest temperature was 28°C at night and 35°C during the day, cooler than Bangkok.

Earlier when we left the beach in the morning a photographer had taken photos, and he wanted us to buy them on return. Ours were such rubbish and £2, we both said no thank you, much to his disgust!

When we returned to the hotel there were papers written in English; one story was that there had been a bomb scare in a Bangkok hotel where we had stayed. A second small hotel had a bomb explode on the premises.

Walking in the streets was no problem; we did not feel under any threat, of mugging or otherwise.

Rosemary had a stomach upset owing to lying in the sun too long. The mosquitoes had been active during the evenings; I had so many bites on my legs. The last evening before our departure, the girls who looked after our rooms brought us each a perfumed rose. This I managed to keep in my sponge bag to return to England.

The weather looked grim with heavy clouds and a possible storm; it was not long before there was thunder. When we awoke in the morning our room was full of perfume from the roses. Outside was a heavy downpour of rain. The minibus collected us and several other people from other hotels to take everyone to Bangkok airport.

It was a six and a half hour flight to Bahrain where the aircraft had to refuel. We had to get off the plane during the refuelling so we had a look round the airport shops, only to find jewellery twice the price of that in Hong Kong, and the articles had probably been made back in Hong Kong!

As usual it was difficult to sleep on the aircraft. We landed at Heathrow Terminal 4, which had only been opened the previous day. Customs men sat with their backs to us as they had gone on strike. Passport control was normal, but the luggage conveyer system was hopeless; we waited a whole hour before retrieving our luggage. Also no one knew anything about where the coaches were and which one went where; tempers were frayed. It was a real shambles. This was certainly a different atmosphere to Asia; I knew we had returned to England!

Australia, New Zealand and Singapore 1987

This was to be an exciting tour as my parents had been to Australia and had also lived in New Zealand; I particularly wanted to see where they had been, having heard so much about their time over there. It was to be a very long haul as we were only stopping for refuelling on the way to Australia. The route from Heathrow took us over Danmark, Latvia and Russia, near Moscow. As we flew over these places we saw snow lying on the ground as this was only March. We then followed on down the Caspian Sea, Nepal and India, leaving Calcutta to cross the sea to Thailand and finally Bangkok; this was 6000 miles from home.

In Bangkok it was 7.30am, 28°C and very humid. While the aircraft was refuelled we visited the duty free area; prices had risen since we had last been here, two years ago. The terminal had been rebuilt and was much larger. After returning to the aircraft, we flew across the China Sea, part of Borneo and Bali to the northern territory of Australia; we had a comfortable flight with plenty to eat. We scrounged free postcards from the crew, which they now no longer offer. Over part of Australia we did encounter some turbulence but as there was a strong tail wind we arrived early at Sydney airport.

At Sydney airport police and their 'sniffer dogs' checked all hand luggage for drugs. We placed the luggage in the middle of the floor and then stood back while the dogs worked. This time nothing was found. Outside a minibus was waiting to take us to the hotel; it did a tour round, dropping people off at various hotels. We finally arrived at 10pm, absolutely exhausted; I had only had about two hours' sleep in the last 36 hours. After falling into bed I knew no more until 9.30 the next morning. I will never travel all this distance again without a break of a day or two en route. Sydney is 10,000 miles from England.

The hotel had been booked from England so we did not know it was in the red light area! At least there was nothing wrong with the hotel, as it was a flag hotel. Breakfast was served in an adjoining cafe. There was plenty of food, so not much was required for the remainder of the day.

Rosemary met friends so I walked down to the central quay and had a Cook's tour of the harbour, including most of the bays. This lasted for an hour and a half; it surprised me how many islands there were in the harbour. Many people seem to speak of Botany Bay as being in Sydney; it is not; it is further along the coastline. This is where people were deported to from England in the bad days, for their misdemeanours. Some of the information collected on the tour was interesting: the revolving tower is 1000 feet high and was built in 1981; Government House has the longest botanical gardens; Sydney Bridge was completed in 1931 and stands 134 meters high. This was the bridge my parents spoke about when reminiscing on their visit to Australia in 1933.

I met up with Rosemary and her friends and we had lunch at a café under umbrellas outside. It was more like Paris. One thing I remember about the place was the gorgeous real apricot drink. In 1996 my neighbour Dennis and I returned here to taste the special apricot juice.

From the café we were taken to the railway station, only to find we had missed the train. The next one was later in the day, so we spent time shopping in a large store which was close by.

The later train was a double decker; both decks were for passengers. It was also the famous 'cross-country' to Perth, stopping at small stations on the outskirts of Sydney. This would take two days to arrive in Perth, on the western coast of Australia. We alighted at one of the small places by the name of 'Springwood'; this was in part of the Blue Mountains. More friends of Rosemary's were waiting for us at the station, Olive and Jim, and took us to their home where we stayed for three days. They made us so welcome and took us out and around the area. An evening meal contained Australian lamb, served with a squash. During the night I could hear the cicadas clicking, like crickets, and bullfrogs croaking, in the woodland surrounding the garden.

Even before breakfast the weather was gorgeous, so we went to explore the garden where oranges and lemons were growing. Rosemary had a swim in their pool, but our hosts said it was too cold at 19°C. (That is the temperature of our sea at home during the summer months!) All the outside doors and windows had a mesh to stop insects coming in. Olive and Jim remarked on how cold it was; we were in summer clothes!

A little Chihuahua called Chico began to make friends with me, sitting on my lap before the day was gone; it was a rescued animal, having had a bad home.

A drive in the car and Jim took us to Katumba. There we saw Echo Valley, which is 3000 feet deep. Rail cars and lifts were available to transport people up and down the deep cliffs. Cotoneaster was growing in the wild, and many eucalyptus trees filled the valley. The trees give off a blue haze, hence the name 'Blue Mountains'. The haze is caused by gasses being released from the trees, so when fires start the gas ignites very quickly and burns furiously. Three famous rocks which can be seen from the top are called 'the three sisters'; they stand very stately and high. Some people try to climb them.

Further on the tour we passed a large lake with a number of birds swimming on the surface. Peach trees were growing wild, and some large lilies grew at the edge of the lake. It is said one country's weeds are another country's prize plants and flowers! There were many bottlebrush trees, which are beautiful when in bloom and also grow to great heights.

We visited Jim and Olive's daughter and son-in-law. They had a delightful home which had been designed and built by them, something that would be out of reach financially in England, but cheap in Australia. It cost £25,000 and that included the land; at the time of writing it would have cost at least £130,000 or more. There was much more opportunity for people here than back in England. This applied to work as well as housing. The son-in-law was training to be an estate agent. The bungalow backed onto a wood and it was here I heard my first kookaburra in the wild. As we left it was getting dark and the cicadas were chirruping.

It was now time to take the train back to Sydney, and we stayed at the university hotel. This place was very noisy in the early morning as lorries were not allowed into town over the weekend; they all seemed to have parked outside our hotel for an early start Monday morning. From about 2am it was impossible to sleep, the engines were so powerful.

A taxi took us to Sydney airport, which was some distance north of the town. Here it was time to fly further north to Cairns. Breakfast was on board and three and a half hours later we arrived. As a point of interest it takes seven hours to fly from Sydney on the east coast to Perth on the west; that just gives one an idea of the size of the country of Australia.

We were met by Rosemary's daughter Diana and her then-boyfriend. A tour round the town of Cairns first before a cup of coffee on the quay. Diana was a receptionist at a hotel on Mission Beach called 'the Castaways'; this was a few miles south of Cairns. Apparently they had 15 inches of rain in 14 days, and therefore everything grew at a terrific pace. Grass could grow as much as one inch in a day. Heavy rain encouraged the sugar cane to grow as it left a humid heat in its wake; the other main income came from tourists.

Mission Beach was so called as it was a little hamlet housing a religious mission, but in 1917 it was swept away in a typhoon. We were treated to luxury rooms at the hotel; as Diana was the receptionist, they were free of charge to us. The evening meal was arranged and brought to our room by Diana and Dick, her boyfriend. They had accommodation close by, a house on stilts. Under the house was room for the car and utilities such as washing. Upstairs was the living accommodation. One outside wall completely folded back and so was open to the outside. They said they went away for weekends leaving everything open; everyone appeared trustworthy.

The next day we were driven through to Townsville through plantations of bananas, pineapples and sugar cane. The farms had a larger acreage in this region. Diana treated us to a picnic with salad and fresh fruit; this was on the coast by the sea. After this we went to see a film on the coral reef; it was a special theatre where we lay back in our seats and looked at the ceiling, which was the screen. The reefs covered a larger area than England, and part of it had lakes, and this was surrounded by the ocean. Later we travelled by boat to Magnet Island, so called as on Cook's exploration it affected his compass. The white sand was very sharp to bare feet as it was coral. Most of the time there was spent on the beach, but returning to the main land I was seasick, even with just a short distance.

Travelling back by car to the hotel, Dick named the many islands along the coast; for most of them one had to obtain a permit to land, as they were in a conservation area. It was very humid as we passed many mango swamps containing trees that grew ferns on the branches. Cassowaries, guinea fowls and cockatoos could be seen at times. Around the doors at the hotel small geckos could be seen. Although Dick kindly gave a commentary as we travelled, not much registered with me; being sick and a migraine did not help. As soon as we arrived back at the hotel I went to bed!

The following morning we were up early for a flight to New Zealand; Dick took us to the airport, taking a different route so we were able to see as much as possible in the short stay. We passed through Ingham and saw the Johnson River where crocodiles were often seen. The crocodiles were invading Cairns and becoming a nuisance; they bred prolifically, but were protected. Some were being caught and transferred to other areas for the safety of the public.

The flight to New Zealand was four hours and ten minutes to Auckland, passing down the east coast of Australia and over Norfolk Island.

Yet more friends of Rosemary met us at the airport and took us by car to Manurewa, a suburb of Auckland. After the evening meal a tour of the lights of town by car was arranged. Next morning I looked round their garden where kiwi fruit grew, not yet quite ripe to eat, and both oranges and grapefruit were already being picked. There was a lovely variety of flowers primarily for flower arranging. Ivy leaf geraniums were climbing an archway so must have been several years old. Busy Lizzies growing at the front of the house were over two feet tall. A beautiful jacaranda tree stood majestically at the entrance to the drive. No late night for us as another early morning was on the schedule. Rosemary's friends were unable to have us stay longer, although we had been told in England 'stay as long as you like'. We had been booked on a coach tour to see the north; little did we know at the time but although we had to pay out an extra £300, they in fact did us a very good turn!

We stopped at the large satellite station at Warkworth and looked round this place that helped telecommunications around the world, as well as other things which they could not discuss. The Brynderwyn range of hills was very scenic, with beautiful views including flora and fauna. We saw Bream Head and Marsden Point on the way to Whangarei and its marvellous clock museum. There were hundreds of clocks of all sizes and ages, well worth seeing. In fact I have been back there and shown other people.

Dairy farms on the way north had large herds, mostly Jerseys which had docked tails. The tails were no more than eight inches long. I do understand now that that particular process has been stopped. While travelling I heard the couple sitting in front of me start talking about farming using terms I knew only farmers used. I started a conversation and found they were retired farmers; after this at every stop that was made we immediately got together. They were so friendly, so there was a reason for this tour. In fact over a period of years I visited them, taking friends with me, until they died. John died first and four years later, in 1998, Sheila passed on at the age of 93.

One place we stopped at was 'SheepWorld' where they gave demonstrations how to handle sheep with dogs. This is a famous place for tourists to stop for coffee! Our guide next stopped at Paihia to obtain tickets for the following day's boat trip. I said if the sea was going to be rough I was not going; I had had enough of being seasick.

The night was spent at a motel at Haruru Falls. We could see the falls from our bedroom, and as we were on the ground floor stood outside the bedroom listening to the birds of the night. The owl who continually called 'more pork': Mother told me about this bird, as she had lived in New Zealand for seven years. There was an island in the middle of the river which flowed from the falls; birds could be heard calling from there. The moon shone and gave an eerie feeling to the trees on the island. The island was seven kilometres round and contained 500 breeding Kiwis; in other words it was a sanctuary.

The following morning was spent just taking it easy watching and listening to birds etc. The coach took us to a ferry to take us to Russell, which was across the bay. This was one of the old settlers' towns where the English and the Maoris kept fighting; eventually the Maoris burnt the town to the ground. It was rebuilt shortly after the fighting ceased.

. Yes, I did go on the cruise around the Bay of Islands after all! Not all were inhabited. When the Queen and Price Phillip came, they stayed on one of the islands. We anchored off one island and had lunch, and some of the party went down in a submarine to look at the life below the water. Afterwards the boat took us through Pieccies rock; this was a tunnel through the rock, and returning through it, I saw marlin swimming in the water close to the boat. Round the side was a cave and this echoed the sound of the engines. This tour took most of a sunny day. The skipper on the boat acted as guide; he had been a lighthouse keeper off Bream Head, but now it was unmanned but still working. In the past any goods required had to be hauled up the cliff as the building was 400 feet high. An interesting day! We returned to the same hotel for the evening.

We paid a visit to Waitangi House, where the main treaty was signed between the Maoris and the 'whites', as it was close to the hotel. This was a wooden house with 'Meeting House' on the door. The meeting house to the Maoris is an important building where they worship and sing. This place was built in 1940, a hundred years after the treaty. The carvings inside were prolific and told stories of the past. Apparently the Maoris used to wait for the whites to cultivate the land around and then want to take it back. As soon as they retrieved the land they let it go back to what it was, letting nature take over, and it returned to scrub.

There was a Maori longboat in a shelter close to the water; 80 men would sit in it and paddle to cross the sea or river. It was made from the wood of the kauri tree, a tree native to New Zealand. We then went on to the museum boat called the *Tui*. Divers had retrieved articles from wrecks along the nearby coast. The finds dated back to the early nineteenth century and consisted of jewellery, personal items including shoes and china.

After the tour left this area we continued along the coast north where the scenery was beautiful, hills, vales and bays. The coach stopped at Kerikeri at a store made of stone, built in an English design and a favourite stopping place for tourists. At Kaeo there were waterfalls, 27 metres high.

The next night was spent at Kaitaia, very pleasant place with Maoris doing the cooking. They are very good cooks. Rosemary and I looked out the window and saw piles of paua shells. She persuaded the kitchen staff to allow her to have some of the shells to bring home. That night roast beef was on the menu and such large helpings for everyone! This stands out as being the best meal on this tour.

The next day's trip took us among orchards with various fruits. The fruit is very prolific in the north of the island, as it is the warmest part of the country. Our driver was Scottish and he had not lost his accent, but enjoyed touring the area with tourists. He took us to Houhora Heads; there was a pretty estuary leading into the Pacific Ocean. There was also a modern museum with modern washing machines and household goods, all working. The history of New Zealand post-European settlement only goes back to 1833, not like our English.

As we travelled further north there was more and more scrubland; this belonged to the Maoris. At least it contained a large amount of wildlife. The estate at Cape Reinga was out of the Maori area and had 22,000 acres for 2000 sheep and 4000 cattle. The Cape itself was interesting as it was where the Pacific and the Tasman Sea met, while a lighthouse overlooked the waves meeting and washing against one another; we were given time to watch this as we picnicked on the side of the cliff. Later in the coach we travelled down the bed of a tidal stream. The driver had to watch where he went as in places there was quicksand; it would have been easy to get the coach stuck here.

To give tourists an unusual ride we were taken down in the coach onto the Ninety Mile Beach, so called; it was only 57 miles long! We alighted at a patch of rocks, where we found some pretty seashells and some fishermen were fishing. Fish were being hauled in. Here the coach firm gave us all an Easter egg, then the following morning the hotel gave us another!

Driving along the sand took us an hour and a half, and the beach was almost deserted. After coming off the beach we had a cup of coffee at the café. While looking out the window we saw the coach was being washed off to stop the salt contaminating the body of the coach. It was specially built underneath to cope with this type of driving.

We then returned to the original coach and were conveyed back to the hotel where we had stayed the previous night. We learnt that Maoris were the proprietors, and they could certainly be well recommended. During the evening entertainment was laid on with Maori singers and dancers, all in national costume. I knew several songs as Mother used to sing them to me when I was a child, so I joined in the singing in Maori.

Yet another early start after a late night talking to the farmer friends. They invited us to come back and stay with them the next time we visited New Zealand! We left Kaitaia after a call at the baker's for some fresh bread rolls for lunch. They cost the equivalent of £1, which was cheaper than the cafés en route. We travelled down the west coast but the roads had many hairpin bends and this upset the stomachs of some passengers. Lovely scenery! The road was shingle and had only just been opened after a cyclone; several sides and banks had been washed away with the heavy rains.

Eventually we stopped at Waipoua forest, a special nature reserve; it was here the largest kauri trees grew. One had a girth of 22 feet at the base, and stood at 150 feet high. It was a beautiful wood with moss and ferns growing on the branches. The tall ponga fern was also there, standing anything from 10 to 20 feet tall, like trees with only leaves at the top. On the banks of the Wairoa River, we chose to eat our picnic lunch; this was at Dargaville. The water was very sandy as the tide had stirred the water as it came in.

The tour firm had chosen the Settlers hotel at Whangarei for the night. We had good company with Sheila and John, the farmers, as we felt that we had known them a very long time, and we had a lot in common. Next day a boat trip took us to Kawau Island; this was where Governor Sir George Grey had lived. It was a beautiful island; the tui bird was calling as we took our time walking through the wood, looking at the sights. These included the smaller island close by where they once mined coal under the sea. When this was discovered the mines were flooded, to stop people working in the mines. This island consisted of 5000 acres, and the Grey house had been kept as a museum with the rooms just as they used to be when Sir George lived there.

Our lunch was provided on the boat as we cruised round the island, enjoying the views of the various bays. The government still retained 10% of the island and the remainder had been purchased by ordinary people. Some of the houses were second homes, and even had helicopter pads. It was no great distance to Auckland when we said goodbye to our farmer friends, agreeing to keep in contact and possibly see them again. This part of the holiday had come to a close!

Rosemary's friend took us round part of Auckland including the university. We found a sheltered spot to enjoy our lunch, close to the hospital. Later that day we collected a 'motor home' to be able to see more of the country.

Motor home we travelled in for part of New Zealand

First stop was Tauranga was 115 miles away and situated in a bay. Here we met a couple from Ringwood in England. They had a photographic shop, and we agreed to meet them in their summer home which was almost on the beach. The flat overlooked the sea, and they lived here for six months of the year and then spent six months in England. The whole afternoon was spent talking about New Zealand and various places to visit. We booked into a campsite on Fifth Avenue for the night and plugged into the electricity which was available for all motor homes, something I had not seen before. We had use of the kitchens for cooking our meal, filling our water tank and checking the fridge for bottle gas.

Hamilton, a few miles away, was the next destination, where I visited the Cattle Breeding Centre. I discussed many topics connected with farming and breeding; a most interesting time. I gathered as much information as possible as I had to give a talk after returning to England.

Young bulls did not necessarily have to be entirely pure to be considered pedigree, just as long as on the dam's side they could be traced back for four generations. Many bulls here were much smaller than the English bulls of the same breed. The mothers were only two years old when the bulls were born. Farmers locally were asked to try the semen of these bulls to help prove them, but they were paid no bonus like the English farmers were for the calf born. The milk recording department and breed societies were in the same buildings. This made it easier for details to be exchanged. Recording in the dairy herds was carried out with New Zealand meters. The average number of cows in the herd was 140, but some farmers had to diversify to help financially; one farm we visited had race horses, others had kiwi fruit and sheep. Cell count testing was found to be a necessity for the herds; back in England this was not yet being used in connection with recording. In fact, due to the details I brought back from my visit, it was decided to commence the cell count testing back home. Lunch was kindly provided in the staff canteen. After this visit we drove south!

We visited the famous Waitomo caves; these were deep underground, with some caverns being very large. There were stalactites and stalagmites in many stages of growth. A boat took us to see the glow worms, where it was completely dark except for the glow of the larvae; there were thousands of them. The guide pulled us along in the boat by a rope fixed to the ceiling.

These glow worms are the larvae of a fly, and remain in this state for nine months; they are then in a chrysalis for a few weeks, emerging as an insect with six legs and wings but no mouth. They reproduce during three days and then die!

We chose a scenic route to Rotorua which took us across country, up and down hills, round winding roads, often with a sheer drop beside us into valleys; it was a beautiful area. This town of Rotorua was the largest we had seen since Auckland. It was significant as my parents had lived there for some time before returning to England in 1933. I found Pukaki Street where they had lived; they had owned a bakery business on a road leading out of town, but here the area had been completely transformed. It was a large dual carriageway with hotels and they now had thermal pools. On entering the town the first thing we noticed was the steam rising from the drains, and also the strong smell of sulphur. We parked on the outskirts of the town at a place called 'Rainbow Fairy Springs': a complex for parking motor homes with a small bird sanctuary and a trout pond. The sanctuary had kiwi birds, which were in darkened houses as they are night birds, and paradise ducks; they pair for life. Trout were of various sizes and enjoyed being fed. A shop on site had stocks of food and gifts for tourists. I decided to walk out to the road and opposite was a 'hot mud pool'; it was interesting watching it bubble away like boiling porridge! Different parts of the pool came to the surface with a 'plop' every few minutes, quite fascinating!

An evening tour took us back to the town and to the government gardens. We were told there was a Maori concert in several places so it was time to look round. After stopping for information we found the meeting house. It was actually where Mother and Father had been at Ohinemutu; I was delighted as I had heard so much about this meeting house and Mother and Father singing with the Maoris. When parking the car we had to be careful as there was a patch of boiling mud nearby. I had been told that it was in such places as this that the Maoris cooked their meals.

On entering the meeting house we were greeted and asked from where we had come. I explained about Mother and Father and mentioned some of the names of guides they had known; they were extremely interested and we talked for some time. I taped the evening concert, and quite unexpectedly I was called to the front of the audience, and what I had told the guide at the beginning was repeated to everyone. The Maoris dedicated their next song to Mother: *Poi Porotiti the Kootuku*. Afterwards a photo of a Maori and myself was taken by a guide. There was one thing which spoilt it: she had her hair dyed auburn instead of having her natural black hair.

Inside a Maori meeting house

The following morning we went to the Maori settlement at Whakarewarewa; apparently I even pronounced the name correctly! I had heard it mentioned so many times in my life. The Maoris charged an entrance fee, and I was able to meet relations of the guides I had mentioned the previous night, such as Guides Mary, Tina and Rangi. The people now in charge were daughters and nieces of the people Mother and Father knew. In the settlement I found the grave of Metatapoki, their chief, whom Mother knew well. Now a large arts and crafts section had been made, including a college. Maoris entered the college, learnt their crafts and were able to return to their village and teach other

47

people the crafts. Guide Mimi took us to see their meeting house and longboat and then on to the 'porridge' pool, where mud just kept turning over.

Mother told me of a gentleman who started courting a Maori girl, and the Maoris did not approve; they preferred to keep to their own race, and not mix with 'whites'. One night he was taking the girl home close to the porridge pool; he was never seen again! It was thought a Maori had pushed him into the pool! The pool was ten feet deep, and had a temperature of 95°C!

Boiling mud pool beside a road

A stream ran through the settlement only three feet wide, but one side was boiling and the other completely cold. In another place steam was coming out of the ground; people were standing and watching. This was Pohutu, also known as the 'Three Feathers', a famous geyser, and every hour it plays hot water and steam 40 feet high into the air for just a few seconds.

Some Maoris were on strike for better pay; groups of them stood at the side of the road to demonstrate. In New Zealand most shops close from Saturday midday until Monday morning.

Finally we said goodbye to Rotorua and all it meant to me. Rosemary drove us on to Taupo; here we had rain and gale force winds. It was not possible to stop for photographs.

As we neared Napier the scenery again was very beautiful, with hills and masses of pine forests; with the rain it smelt so very fresh. I hung on to the side as we were travelling at 90 km per hour instead of 60! Not my driving!

Napier was three and a half hours' journey, and we soon found my aunt's bungalow. Mother knew her as a girl; she was now in her seventies and looked just like my great-grandmother. She was very pleased to see us; we were made very welcome and enjoyed the meal she placed before us. Rosemary went to find the park for the campervan and left us talking about the family the whole evening. Mother had sent gifts and a message on tape.

Rosemary by now had found the park a few yards down the road. We managed to carry on the exchange of news with Auntie; unfortunately she was one of those people who must worry about everything. I had met her daughter in England during the 1950s. Her son was in Papua New Guinea and she was going to visit him the following week. We enjoyed the two days spent with her, not long but we had so much to see!

As we were on tour we had a deadline to meet at Christchurch, so we travelled on.

Wellington was the next stop; we had been informed it was 'a wet and windy Wellington'. This was found to be true. The land was mostly flat on the way there, and it took us five and a half hours. It was 4pm when we caught the ferry to Picton, South Island. There was quite a swell on the sea, but I managed without being seasick: no extra food for the fish.

By this time it was dark; it had been a lovely sunset. We drove on to Blenheim for somewhere to stay. We wanted to park so that we could connect up to the electricity; it was frosty, South Island being much cooler than the north.

The next day we made our way to Nelson; in one place it was a shingle road, and another road was flooded with water. The main roads in South Island are more like our secondary roads back home. The roads only improve when getting near a town. There was very little traffic, and we were lucky if we saw three or four cars an hour. We had to remain on the main roads as far as possible, as the owners of the campervan were a little bit particular and did not want any damage. Actually any damage would have cost us a 'bomb'.

Ayers Rock from the air

Nelson was a busy town with a large amount of building being carried out. We continued on to Stoke, Richmond and Brightwater, where my parents had lived when they had first come out to New Zealand. Mother worked in the apple orchards making the boxes. We saw many orchards still in the vicinity after so many years: they had been here in 1927. We continued our circuit back to the east coast, where there were more hills, hairpin bends and gorgeous scenery. The river ran along the bottom of the valley, and it was possible to see where the water rose after heavy rains. It was clear that rains had not fallen for some time as the hills were scorched brown. The road on the coast was very straight; one could see for miles. To the west were high volcanic mountains and some of the old lava had turned to black sand on the beaches.

We settled for the night at Seddon; it was quiet and some distance from the main road. There we decided to prepare the next day's food; to anyone outside it probably smelt good as it was steak and onions, carrots, parsnips and potatoes. A jelly was also made and put in the fridge; it had time to set before we moved off in the morning. As expected we had a frost overnight.

On leaving Auckland we had been presented with a large bag of apples, kiwi fruit and passion fruit. Rosemary left me to eat most of the fruit; I had lived on these while she ate things such as buns and cakes. During the evening we sorted out our finances, and how much we had left to spend on food.

We followed the number one highway; this took us mostly along the coast, passing deer farms with high fences. The traffic was still minimal and we were told that only a third of the population lived in South Island. In one place we drove over a mountain pass with narrow and winding roads. Quite a different type of scenery from the north; all the hills were dry and brown, no running water in the creeks. We stopped at a small bay and were the only people there.

In the morning we woke to the sound of the bellbird singing; this was 30 kilometres from Christchurch. As I lived near the Christchurch of England I had to have a look round the town. I spent time at the large cathedral and found a duty free shop where I purchased some paua shell earrings.

We booked in at the Commodore hotel as we had to give up the campervan; we had come to the end of the tour, and at the time predicted, having enjoyed our time. We cooked our last meal in the 'Customs Staff' park, then finally returned the home to the depot adjoining the airport.

During our tour we travelled 2004 kilometres in seven days. Petrol cost £53.36; this was cheaper than the coach tour in North Island. We also stopped and saw what we wanted, not being told what to see and how many minutes we had. I thoroughly enjoyed the freedom and would like to do something like this again.

There was fog on the runway when we took off and as we were leaving we could see snow on the mountains down the centre of South Island; the pilot flew lower than normal so that we could enjoy the beauty of the Alps.

We eventually arrived in Singapore after a stop in Melbourne, where Rosemary met another friend while we waited for our connecting flight. The following morning a coach took us on a tour of Singapore. The guide informed us the population was 2 million and that three quarters were Chinese, 10% Indian, 3% Malaysian and 1% of mixed race. Malay was the main language. One stop was at the Tianfu Gong Temple, but this was in a very dilapidated state. People walked amongst those praying and various things being sold, such as pictures, slides and postcards. I felt this was much like the story in the Bible when Jesus cast the people out of the temple. Houses around the area were in great need of repairs; it was obvious that little money was available. We left there and went to one of the highest points on the island, Mount Faber Park; from here we could see the cable cars leaving and crossing to Sentosa Island. The harbour below us was one of the busiest in the world, a boat leaving every three minutes.

Education for children was not compulsory, though many attended part-time. Schooling was five and a half days a week, one group attending mornings and another afternoons. National service was compulsory for boys for three years, while many girls did voluntary work. Not many old cars were on the road as the road tax doubled after they were ten years old. Petrol at this time was the equivalent of 20 pence per litre.

The Botanic Gardens were very interesting; there many types and colours of orchids were grown. While we were there a bride and groom came to have their photographs taken; we understood this was a common event. There were large beautiful coloured butterflies flying around in the gardens. As usual we were taken to a shopping plaza; the drivers had their own special places to take visitors, where they gained commission. This was not always the best place to shop! We asked to be taken to the Lucky Plaza as this was a better place to shop.

After this a taxi took us back to the hotel, but we soon found the fee they charged had to be discussed before moving off! The driver tried to increase the price as we travelled along. In the end we paid him after we got out what he had first asked and said we had no more! I do not think he was very pleased. That evening a coach returned us to Changi airport.

A piece of information we gathered was that if cars were not full at the busiest time of day in the centre of Singapore, owners could be heavily fined. Four traffic police stand at traffic lights checking the number of people in a car. We also learnt that the emblem of Singapore is a lion – a lion's head and a fish tail.

There is a monument standing on the quay which was built in 1972 by a local craftsman. It is compulsory for everyone of age to vote; if they do not they are automatically struck off the electoral roll and have to reapply to be eligible to vote again.

On the way home we flew to Bombay, but did not get off the aircraft; eventually we arrived back in Heathrow feeling rather jetlagged! It was all worthwhile as it was a very enjoyable holiday, and one I would be prepared to take again.

Making friends

Germany, Austria and Switzerland
July 1991
(three weeks)

This was a very early start; we had to leave home at 4am and to travel by taxi, as we lived many miles from Heathrow. From here we flew to Stuttgart. But this time there were three of us. We had to pay for a trolley to put our luggage on. My neighbour Dennis and I travelled with his 15-year-old daughter Anthea.

The car hire was only yards away from where we landed, but the car we were hiring had been returned late by the previous customer, so we waited until it was cleaned. We asked for directions out of the airport on to the motorway, but the people we asked, it turned out, did not know left from right and gave us wrong directions; we ended up returning to where we had started!

Dennis decided to drive and turned east when we finally found the motorway. We stopped for a cup of coffee and found a nature reserve for buzzards. Many of the birds were gliding overhead and over the wood. Later in the town of Ulm we walked along the side of the river and looked across to the large church; it has a very high steeple and this stood above the other buildings; a beautiful town.

I had not booked any overnight stay, so we kept going until we felt it time to stop. We drove through Menningen to a village called Moos. Here we found a place with a swimming pool, and a super view of the Alps from our bedroom window. We were on the border of Germany and Austria, staying in a guest house that offered bed and breakfast. The owners told us of a hotel not far away for a main evening meal. It was very memorable as there were stuffed heads of animals all round the restaurant at picture rail height. The animal heads were of various species, from deer to badger and polecat; it certainly started conversations. An enjoyable meal, but Anthea and I were tired and so went to bed early. Dennis stayed up and found an English couple to talk to, now living in Switzerland, so he enjoyed the evening.

Bed and breakfast

We did not rise early the next morning, but eventually went down for breakfast. The mist and low cloud hung over the nearby mountains, so we decided we would not rush away. The weather cleared and it became a lovely sunny day. We walked along the side of the lake opposite where we were staying, taking our time to admire the scenery. We eventually left this tranquil area and drove on to Füssen and over the borders into Austria. We stopped many times to admire the beautiful scenery. We used the cameras and captured this for happy memories.

After driving through several villages, we came to gorgeous fresh water gushing out of the hillside and had a drink. The mountain side was very steep, and then there were deep gorges opposite. Dennis had been to Berwang before, so we stopped to enjoy the flora and fauna, as numerous spring flowers were in bloom. It was lovely to see gentian with bright blue flowers in among the rocky areas. I had seen some at home but seeing them in their natural state was more exciting. Birds were singing their spring songs in the pine trees, which also smelt beautiful; it all helped to build the picture that I had only imagined in the past.

There were many miles to travel, so was time to move on again. Driving back to Lermos we could see Zugspitze, a mountain point that stood 2983 metres high. A café was at an appropriate position for people to have a cup of coffee and an apple strudel, and to look out at the mountain. We looked down into one of five lakes in the Fern Pass; the water was almost black where it was at its deepest, and a bright turquoise round the shallow edge.

We drove down the Pass to the castle and hotel; there were tourist shops open for us to browse. Most of the villages were tucked into the side of mountains, but we decided to return to Moos again for the second night. The hotel served some very tasty food.

Hohenschwangau Castle was the destination we aimed for next day. Most of the contents of the castle date back to 1812, as Nelson destroyed it earlier; it has since been rebuilt. The castle is now open to the public, so we were able to see the carvings and period furniture. There is a long winding road to the top of the hill where it stands; there were great views overlooking a lake.

Later we visited another castle which stands on a hill opposite Hohenschwangau. Neuschwanstein was the name of this second castle. The two castle names mean 'High Swan' and 'New Swanstone'; everywhere there is the insignia of a swan. In the grounds of Neuschwanstein stood a high footbridge called 'Maria Theresa Brocke'; this straddled a deep gorge above the castle. This castle was built later and I felt it was the much more interesting of the two. The wood panelling and architecture were more noticeable, and the steep climb to it was really worthwhile. It decided to pour with rain when we came out, so we took a horse and trap down to the car as this was under cover. We returned to Moos, where snow had fallen on the tops of the mountains.

Next morning we opened the curtains only to find more snow had fallen overnight. It was time to move on to the next 'Zimmer' (room), so now a visit into town to purchase some lunch and visit the bank was in order. My Barclaycard was not accepted; I was told to visit a larger town for money. En route we drove along the side of a lake and then to Linderhof Castle. This seemed very popular as we had to join a long queue to enter. It was worth the wait as the castle was more ornate and interesting than the previous two. We walked in the gardens up to the grotto, only to find that it was very artificial. We left here for Innsbruck, stopping at the small village of Scharnitz, where we found a small guest house. We had passed a pub on the way there so we went back for the evening meal. I remember they advertised trout on the menu, and this was a favourite of Dennis's.

The next morning our flask was filled with hot water, for a cup of soup and a cup of coffee to take with us. Our breakfast before leaving was just continental. We drove through Zirl and Telfs, past the Stams Monastery to Motz, where we looked inside the church. The altar and pulpit were made of wood, but highly painted and looked more like marble. There was a lot of decoration in the church and the sun shone through the windows, making the most of the inside. There was a large statue of Christ standing in the sunlight. We also visited the Church of Maria Locherboden, which was on the highest hill in the area and therefore could be seen for miles around. As Dennis had been in the area before he wanted to stop at a hotel in Silz, but he could not get a response and the place was dilapidated, I think he had an idea to stay there as he had in the past. The local shop said the hotel was closed.

The next place of interest was Oetz; we climbed along the side of a stream, between pine trees and snow, only to see a man chopping wood for logs. Dennis remembered him from a previous visit, so stopped and talked to him; he spoke English. Dennis was delighted to have a long talk with him, about the area and how it had changed over the past 15 years. We also spent time watching the stream for trout. At the top of the hill, snow lay around, and Anthea slid down the hill on a plastic bag, as we had no skis!

Travelling down the other side of the hill we saw a chamois close to the road; it stood for a while before dashing higher up the mountain. We then found a secluded spot by a stream, where we stopped for a picnic lunch and watched fish swimming in the water.

Driving on again, we eventually came to Innsbruck to find some money from one of the banks. No one except the Central Bank would oblige. I had travelled in many countries and never had my card refused before.

Exploring the following day we found the Europa Bridge, which was further south. Also the Igls (Eagles) ski resort, where the winter Olympics had once been held; we travelled on a cable car to the summit. This was 6405 feet high. Sitting outside the café in the sun was so warm, although snow was on the ground. We sat in sleeveless shirts. Flowers were all around us so we examined some, a white flower with blue veins and the shape of a crocus; also we found edelweiss.

After returning to the village, and visiting a few shops, we followed on to another village called Patch. This was where we booked in to a farm house for the night. The place was spotlessly clean. Our bedrooms were over the cattle; I could hear them in the night, but both Dennis and Anthea slept soundly, with Dennis snoring! In the morning I went down to the sheds and spoke to the farmer about his animals; he was busy hand milking when I arrived.

Later in the day we found narrow roads which went up to the mountains. We found a safe place to park and walked. The air was so clean and fresh, with lovely views. Who wants to walk in smoky towns after this? So much of this holiday cannot be put on paper, as looking, watching and walking took up a considerable amount of time. Much of the scenery was not easy to describe, with views of mountains, hillsides and lakes; each was different. Cattle bells could be heard close by as well as in the distance. To quote a certain musical: 'the hills are alive with the sound of music'.

In the evening we took a walk around the village of Patch, where a brass band was playing; this was the second night we had heard it, so we decided to find where it came from. They were practising in the local village hall. I listened outside for some time.

The Frau at the house was a good cook and gave us plenty of food; she also filled the thermos flask for the daily trip. This time we went to Stams Monastery. It was worth staying some hours looking around the very decorative roof and walls. There was a considerable amount of wrought iron work, probably made in Germany. The entry gates into the monastery had so many scrolls in the design, it must have taken a lot of patience to have made them, with hours of work; they were used to their advantage.

Sunday was the next morning, with a very misty start to the day; the tops of the mountains were not visible, then suddenly the mist disappeared and we could see the valleys. We decided to visit Alpenzoo on the outskirts of Innsbruck; there were many different animals and birds, not all native to Austria. We returned to Patch for a change of clothes; we thought we should look more respectable for the evening meal. There was only one place open, it being Sunday; it was expensive, but it was holiday time, so what?

After the meal we returned to the village; the oompah band was playing and people were dancing. The music was very lively, with a toe-tapping rhythm.

The following morning we packed our suitcase and moved on in a westerly direction, passing Landeck and up to the Silvretta Dam, which was situated in a mountain pass. Water was piped through the tunnel in the mountain to the other side over a distance of two and a half kilometres. The other side was all downhill with 23 hairpin bends in the road; each one was numbered. This took us down to the bottom on the other side of the pass. As we were so high up, it rained the whole time so we could not experience any of the views.

Leaving this behind we entered Liechtenstein, and to Valduz to see the royal castle (at a distance). We had left the mountains behind and now only had small hills. Liechtenstein was small: only 60 square miles. This was now a farming area with 40 or 50 cows per farm, and many working horses in the fields.

It was into Switzerland we went next, stopping near Lake Constance; here we stayed in a flat above a shop. Everywhere was in pinewood, more of a Swedish design, but very cosy. We cooked all our meals during our stay here as all utensils needed were available. The food came from the local village.

In Konstanz, time was spent looking round shops and comparing prices, particularly in the music shop. Dennis was interested in some electronic organs, and I found some accordion music. I could have remained in there all day. In an adjoining road a street artist was busy on the pavement in chalk. He had drawn the face of a person and it was perfect, it looked so lifelike. Round the corner were two accordion buskers playing classical music. This drew a large crowd as they played so well, really professional. On the way back to the flat we stopped and browsed in an antique shop, silver, furniture and paintings. It contained so much, it was difficult walking through.

The next day it was packing again and preparing for a long journey to Heidelberg; having seen the film that was made in the locality, I had said at the beginning of the holiday this stop was a must. The castle looked very appealing, especially with the memory of *The Student Prince*. Before arriving we came across Schaffhausen Falls and felt we had to stop there; they were very wide and appeared in full spate. It had been raining heavily in Northern Germany and the water had now reached the falls.

We found a spot to stop and had lunch while watching the falls. Pleasure boats were sailing around the base of the falls; sooner them than me!

View of Heidelberg including castle

Later in the day we had to drive north of Heidelberg to obtain accommodation. We drove round and round trying to find somewhere; most places were full or had the wrong type of bedroom for us. Few people could speak English, which did not help. Eventually a guest house was found. As a student was away we were able to have his room and one other. A lovely view across the valley from our window.

The evening meal was at a small place just down the road with home cooking. At the next table was a German family; the husband was a journalist and he had travelled the world reporting on films, theatre and books. As the family were leaving, the daughter gave Anthea a serviette, with her name and address written on it, and asked Anthea to write to her, as they were the same age.

The next morning it was very misty over the hills, so we took our time before driving in to the town. We parked near the river Neckar and watched some locks open and shut for the larger boats to sail through; barges and tourists' boats were passing through at the side. The river was very busy with the various craft. We watched a yellow wagtail; it came to us for titbits.

We went shopping in the town before going to the castle where *The Student Prince* was filmed. The castle dated back to 1300, with many old buildings in the grounds. Unfortunately the day we arrived the castle was closed; we just walked in the gardens as we could not go in. The birds were singing in the woods as we toured the area. I was a little disappointed as this was somewhere I really wanted to see.

We stayed one more night at the same lodgings, made ourselves tidy before going to the same restaurant as the previous night. The steak we chose came from a farm close by and was so tender. There was only one more complete day before returning home. We said farewell to Frau, who offered Anthea a room should she ever think of coming to the university.

This time we followed the river valley; so pretty, I would love to return there. The river was very busy, and there were many vineyards en route; the area is very famous for its wine, much of which is exported all over the world. On the outskirts of Stuttgart we found a bed and breakfast, where we stayed the night and enjoyed the evening.

The following morning was an early breakfast and a drive to the airport. It was not easy to find, as there were no signs until we actually got within sight of the aircraft.

Everything was normal; we were met by a friend at Heathrow and driven back to Ringwood Hants.

This was a very enjoyable holiday, having seen many places of interest, and if possible I would love to return.

Hong Kong, Australia and America
August 1992
(four weeks)

I am not going to cover the complete tour as we visited places I had already been, which in turn we all found very interesting.

Dennis, Anthea and I went to Hong Kong first. Anthea had her hair permed in a hotel hairdresser; it cost Dennis £40 but unfortunately they were not used to coping with European hair, and the perm was not successful. While Anthea was at the hairdresser's Dennis and I went to another part of the island, Cat Street, to see the antiques. We were very disappointed, as we considered it all rubbish, tins, parts of watches, just useless. At the end of the street was a fish shop; how people could buy from there I do not know! It smelt putrid, it made both of us feel sick and we had to stand for a while to let our stomachs settle before moving on; the smell will never be forgotten.

Later Anthea wanted to go on the Star Ferry, so we all crossed together. Before leaving England, we had seen a booklet which suggested shops for tourists to visit. This time we decided to visit the jeweller that had been recommended. We found the address; downstairs it looked very dilapidated, but the jeweller came down to meet us and took us upstairs in a lift. The jewellery was beautiful; the gems came from all over Asia. Because we chose two rings, it was possible to obtain a discount! I bought a beautiful ring with three large zircon stones for approximately £100; I have since had it valued in England for £400. Anthea chose a sapphire that was set in gold and it fitted perfectly. Mine had to be enlarged and was sent direct to England, and saved import tax.

From Hong Kong we flew to Sydney, and during our stay we visited Darling Harbour and the interesting aquarium, where we spent most of the afternoon. There were so many species of fish for everyone to have a good view of as we walked through the tunnel underneath the water, the fish swimming over us. It was as though we were swimming with them!

There was interesting information in the hotel where we were staying regarding Featherstone Park; this was a zoo on the outskirts of Sydney. The next day we decided to go there. We went to Circular Quay and caught a bus; Dennis decided it was the correct one, but we ended up in Botany Bay, several miles from where we should have been! After changing buses we eventually arrived at the park! It was worth it in the end, after a good laugh regarding the roundabout route.

We travelled to Cairns and a passport was not required as we were travelling on an internal flight. There was sufficient time to have a full meal on board. At our destination we hired a car, but it had to be changed as one of the doors would not open, so we ended by having a larger vehicle for the same price. We decided to have a day on the Barrier Reef, so a tour was booked for the following day.

We had a one-day visit, which included stopping at Green Island, as this was part of the coral reef, off the Cairns coast. Tours were run in fairly large boats out to Green Island; on the way there were large marker poles which gave the route for the boats with the right depth of sea. On the top of one of these poles a cormorant was nesting; it had hatched out its young and we saw the chick being fed by the parent.

The first stop was Green Island; the journey had taken an hour. People were on the quay, feeding large fish that jumped out of the water, while we walked along the jetty. The sea was so clear we could see the bottom although it was several feet deep. Close to the actual shore the colour changed to a lovely turquoise.

Many crocodiles had been rescued as they had been a danger in the wild; now they had their own wired-in pens here, with their own ponds, and were safely set apart from humans. Some were as long as 30 feet. Besides the crocs there were many craft shops showing Aboriginal art and also a small aquarium. This was below sea level; we walked into a tunnel, and the fish swam round in their natural environment.

The next move was by jet boat out to the Norman Reef. Here was a large pontoon where more than one boat could be tied, while tourists could look through a glass at the underwater life. Some people dived with oxygen to several feet under water, or snorkelled round the reef, or just stood on the pontoon looking down into the water watching what was happening underneath. Dennis estimated that it was possible to see 40 feet below. A special net was placed round the perimeter to stop sharks coming in to the swimming area, where they could be a danger. There was a large variety of fish which enjoyed the company of people; children and grown-ups were holding on to the large fins, and were being towed around the pool. Anthea said this was the best day of her life, being able to swim with the fish.

Snorkelling on the Barrier Reef

A submarine dive over some of the coral and rocks was part of the day's outing. A free meal was served but being a bad traveller I did not partake, as we had two hours before returning to the shore! Even so this was a special day that none of us would forget.

The next trip was in the car and we drove to the Crystal Falls; these were further north from Cairns, near Kuranda. There was so little water there as rain had not fallen for a long time. The Barron Falls were not worth stopping to see owing to the same reason. Now we drove inland to Mareeba where there were tall termite mounds, anything between six and ten foot high. I remember David Attenborough said how snakes like to get at the base of a mound and hide out of the sun. So we left them well alone!

Malanda on the Atherton Plains was the next stop; when Dennis tried to find accommodation in the hotel there, going inside was like the wild west in America, like the films! So back to Atherton and we went to a motel.

The next venture had me sitting on the edge of my seat! We visited part of the bush near Herberton. Houses were more like shacks, caravans were scattered around in the bush. The deeper we went into the bush the worse the road was, really only fit for 4x4 vehicles. Ours was a new car and I was somewhat worried; any damage done would have to be paid for by myself. I persuaded Dennis to turn back. We had crossed a dry stream as we first drove down, but coming back the bank was too steep for us. We ended up with Anthea going to the first home for help; an Aussie came to our rescue with a Land Rover and pulled us out. The gentleman was in bare feet and had only one eye. Dennis offered to pay him but he refused, saying that he was originally from England.

Now I must put a postscript to this! Anthea lost her wallet in the bush, but was not sure whereabouts. In the November after we arrived home from the tour, a letter arrived from our rescuer to say the wallet had been found a few days after we had been towed in the bush. Anthea's name and address were inside. The gentleman returned the wallet and ALL it contained; this included 300 Australian dollars, which Dennis thought had gone for good. How honest the one-eyed, bare-footed man had been. We talked about him for a long, long while.

Back to Australia! The following day Dennis took me to a farm for a pre-arranged visit. Dennis and Anthea had the day together while I spent time with the farmer learning about

Australian dairy farming. I was taken to several farms, seeing the difficulties the dairy farmers had to endure on the Atherton Plains. As I was still working, it was interesting to talk and gather information to show colleagues at work when I returned home. We stopped at a petrol station for petrol afterwards and met the owner and some of her family, so helpful and pleasant.

Eventually we returned to Cairns; food was cheaper here than in other towns. By now the car had an extra 806 kilometres on the clock, plus a collection of stones in the back bumper from the bush trip, and we gave our final goodbye to Australia.

Hello to New Zealand, after a five-hour flight, and to John and Sheila, the couple I met on my first visit to the country! We were made very welcome; it was the first time they had met Dennis and Anthea. Once again we had a hired car to give us freedom, after a short stay. This time it was a Corolla automatic.

We decided to do a two-day trip up to the Bay of Islands, staying at Wellsford en route. It was so cold we were pleased to return to Auckland. I had in my notes of August 24 that there was a hard white frost. The following morning I was up early to go to a small place called Bombay to travel with a van driver, collecting milk samples from farms with the Farmers' Recording Society. I walked with farmers asking questions about their herds and recording programmes. A milk recorder took me to a farm where she was recording that afternoon, when I gained more interesting information. On returning to Auckland I found John had taken Anthea and Dennis out to the surrounding area for the day.

The following day was another goodbye, this time to our friends and New Zealand, but hello to Los Angeles. Owing to the international date line it was 8pm on August 26 when we departed, and yet we arrived on August 26 at 11.45 am. This had become a very long day. We travelled Air New Zealand; they made our journey comfortable, and we could not fault their food.

I took Anthea to the Universal Studios during the next day as Dennis did not feel well; the change in the temperature had upset him. This was on the northern side of LA. We saw how films were made with some scenes and how they looked real. We saw the tallest building in town, 75 storeys high, and the famous Hollywood sign on the hill. The weather was pleasant but much hotter than New Zealand with the temperature reaching 32°C. During the short stay Dennis spent most of his time in the hotel, as he could not cope with the heat.

On the way home we had the experience of flying with Virgin Airlines; other than having our own TV screens in front of us the journey was not too pleasant. It was difficult to obtain seats together, then a young child was sitting in our line of seats; she was travelling on her own. She kept talking and crying as she had left her father behind, and was to join her mother in England. She was too young to travel that distance on her own for the ten hours. When we returned home I wrote to Richard Branson personally and told him the story, also pointing out some good points. Richard answered with an apology for the problems, and enclosed a cheque for £100.

The final thoughts of this trip: it could have been better but it was very interesting.

At Los Angeles airport

Florida
March 1994
(two weeks)

Rosemary was one of the lucky people to obtain two tickets to Florida through one of the vacuum cleaner companies; many had applied but were not lucky enough to have them. In actual fact we collected ours at Manchester airport on the morning of the flight. We think it was because her solicitor wrote to the firm concerned that the tickets should be supplied to us!

We left Hoylake, Rosemary's home, at 5.15 in the morning to drive to the airport. Our tickets were collected from a special 'book in' desk. The flight had been delayed until 10.15am as the aircraft had been late leaving America. We found we were travelling with Leisure Airbus, the same firm that had provided the tickets, and on a Boeing 767.

When we boarded there were two people not allowed on, as there were problems with their passports. We had to wait for their luggage to be found and removed from the flight. Also there was a maintenance problem, so we missed our slot in take-off. It was finally 11.10am when we left Manchester. The service on board was not so good. Our meals were supposed to be hot but were only warm, and drinks had to be paid for; usually on this length of flight drinks were given to us. At least the flight was free!

Arriving in Orlando lengthened our day as it was 4.45pm on arrival, with a temperature of 29°C. The usual screening of luggage and ourselves was carried out. We travelled by the monorail and finally collected our luggage.

The company organising our trip had a special stand in the foyer and a package which contained general information, including places to visit. We were pleased not to have hired a car as the road regulations were so different, we were happier to travel by bus or taxi.

When we had eventually booked in to the hotel in Orlando, a meal was enjoyed before an American early night (2am English time). Next morning it was very humid weather, more like Hong Kong. The travel information was read from cover to cover before we moved out of bed! We had decided to be lazy and catch up with the time difference.

We spotted a restaurant opposite the hotel where food was considerably cheaper: a full three-course meal with as much as we could eat for £3.80 English money.

Rosemary wanted to spend several days in various parts of Disney World; as this did not appeal to me, I set off to the Everglades and Cape Canaveral, travelling at 8.30am by coach to an area of the St John's river. Here we travelled by hovercraft, wearing earmuffs as the engine was very noisy. Everyone was looking for 'gators': alligators. There were various species of wildlife and I am sure we would have seen more if the hovercraft had been quiet. We came across a man in a small boat who was fishing; I would have loved to be in the boat with him, just sitting, watching and listening.

I had the company of an English man for the day; he said he had travelled the world on his own, but it was interesting to have someone to talk to and discuss the subjects. Just proof you need not be lonely travelling on your own.

After the trip on the river I visited an exhibition at the Kennedy Space Centre. This showed what had been used for space travel, which rockets, and the way space travel had benefited the ordinary people. Pacemakers had been invented, and children who had to be isolated in hospital could have a special clear vision tent while in bed. Quick-frozen and dried foods had also evolved through space travel.

Films were shown of rocket launches and we had a look around the area. A coach took us round to see the launch pads. One pad had seen many launches as well as returns on the runway, including the very first enormous rocket.

Cape Canaveral consisted of 140,000 acres of ground. On the outskirts orange groves had been planted and leased to farmers.

Incidentally the orange tree can bear fruit for up to 100 years. Cacti were along the side of the road, standing several feet high; wildlife was in abundance including eagles, buzzards, egrets and pelicans. One thing we learnt was that an eagle's nest could weigh up to 200 pounds. This was a very enjoyable and interesting day out. Rosemary went to Disney World and stayed to see the laser light display, so when we met in the hotel there was a lot to discuss.

The following day I took a trip to Silver Springs. This was a zoo but had large enclosures for each group of animals; some animals were difficult to see as they were in the further part of the paddocks, some hiding in woodland. The animals had a lot of freedom. I took a trip on the 'Silver Springs River' in a boat as this was the best way to see the animals. There were places where hot water bubbled from the bed of the river; we were told that a spring could fill an Olympic-size swimming pool in two minutes! An island in the river contained monkeys; they were lying on the roof of their shelter enjoying the hot sun. After this a Land Rover took us on a trip through a very large compound to see even more animals. Our entrance tickets covered all the trips, in the boat and Land Rover. The weather had been very kind during the tour around the zoo. It changed as we returned to Orlando with pouring rain. One thing we noticed while travelling along the roads was that when work was being carried out, plastic screens were put up to keep the 'gators' away, for the safety of the workmen.

The scenery as we travelled for an hour and a half was varied and interesting, with orange groves and two or three racehorse studs, all advertised with the stud name at the end of the drive. Many people lived in mobile homes much larger than the ones in England. If they owned some ground they could have permission to put a home on there!

Rosemary's visit that day was to the MGM studios. She was shown a sequence of films made to look real; it sounded interesting.

The following day was Valentine's Day and America makes it very popular with young people, particularly for commercial reasons. Weddings take place on TV, and other people have blind dates organised. For the evening meal we were presented with a red carnation each. The humidity had dropped for the evening so it was more comfortable enjoying the evening meal.

Rosemary and I had heard about the Orange State Fair at Kissimmee. There were no buses so we travelled in a taxi. The temperature was now 23°C with humidity of 39%, much more comfortable and not even a cardigan was required.

All the cattle at the fair were beef breeds, a Brangus (an Aberdeen Angus crossed with a Brahmin), a plain Brahmin, Simmental, Limousin and Hereford cross. We watched the judging of the cattle, which took place in a building with a sand-covered ring. After the judge had made his decision for the prize winners, he took the microphone and explained how and why he had placed them in that order. The class entries were small in comparison to the English county shows, and this was the county show for the Orange State. I spoke to one farmer and he had 63,000 acres and 3000 head of cattle, all beef with Brangus and Brahmin breeds. He won most of the classes we watched.

There was a large fair to occupy the children; this contained roundabouts and various rides. Hot dogs and popcorn, ice cream and baked potatoes were all on sale. One shed had children's competitions, painting, needlework and plants. Another part had adult competitions, painting, needlework, quilting and woodwork, alongside craft stalls selling their wares. One stall was selling tyres for vehicles and at a much cheaper price than England. Most farmers had pick-up vehicles rather than saloon cars. These had room for the whole family inside and had metal boxes on the back, which could be locked while carrying goods. Some of the boxes were the size of some of our deep freezers.

We returned to the hotel with a Dutch girl driving our taxi; she went out of her way to be helpful; in fact we had found everyone very pleasant while in their country. We found our cruise tickets for the Bahamas waiting, which we were to use in a day or two.

The following day was spent in Disney World, with all the cartoon characters. This part of Disney World was enormous. Walt Disney had in fact purchased 30,000 acres. While he was purchasing the land he did so in the name of four or five other firms from all over America to stop any suspicion that he was the buyer. If his name had been known, he would have had to pay much higher prices; as it was he was able to purchase the swamp at £72 per acre! At the beginning an enormous amount of money was spent on draining the land properly, and making lakes.

Disney World, Florida

The entrance of £26 was for the day, but this covered all expenses except food. There were many rides and the chance to meet the great Disney characters and also a grand parade in the afternoon. As soon as we arrived we were taken by motor rail away from the car parks around the perimeter of the park. The actual entrance had 20 turnstiles to enter, saving too many queues. There were also links to visit the other theme parks within the large complex, MGM Studios, Epcot and the Typhoon Lagoon water park; each had an entrance fee of £26.

The first stop was to the Town Hall where we paid for a guide. This was well worth the money; as adults we learnt more about the background to the parks. Walt Disney wanted ordinary people to step into fantasy land and forget everything else for a day. He was also a lover of wildlife, so part of the grounds was kept for nature conservation.

We ventured on to a space ride much like that at the Universal film studios to obtain the atmosphere. Most rides lasted from seven to ten minutes.

We saw the 'Liberty Tree'; this was the largest tree found in the swamp when Walt Disney started to build. It was transplanted to a suitable place. It was 150 years old and weighed 45 tons; it took two weeks to move seven miles. Years ago the Liberty Tree was the equivalent of a town centre, where business was conducted and problems discussed.

A statue had been cast of Cinderella and at certain times of the year when the sun shines a halo forms over her head on the background. The haunted house was an area we visited and brought a discussion on how ghosts could come and go! Walt Disney made the magic with Perspex and reflections. The grand parade was something worth watching with all the various characters and the razzmatazz that went with it. The gardens were kept in perfect condition, with colours of plants used to show flowers at their best. It was an interesting day and something unusual, but not a place with sufficient interest for me to return!

The day had arrived for the cruise; we were taken to Port Canaveral, passing through immigration ready to board the SS *Atlantic*. This was 30,000 tons, 468 feet long and known as the 'Big Red Boat', as it was painted red externally. There were 1400 passengers with 560 crew on board. As we had a last-minute booking we received a large cabin from a cancellation and were only charged for one person! There were two single beds, our own shower and toilet; it was almost as large as a hotel bedroom!

A programme of various educational events was laid on for adults, and we attended these during the cruise. The Red Boat had eight decks and the lowest had a large restaurant. When first joining the boat we went round with a map to find where various events were taking place. A buffet was running most of the day, but proper meals were held at given times. Once the boat had embarked no money was required; food was included in the price, even ice creams were included, but alcohol had to be paid for at the end of the trip. Dinner was well presented with five courses.

After the evening meal I took travel sickness pills as we were warned of a rough night. Passengers were being offered pills by the purser! I slept most of the night, but do remember rolling on the bunk!

Next morning Rosemary and I were up early; the sea had calmed, but only the two of us went to breakfast. We learned that even some of the crew were affected, and over half the passengers had been ill. Various events took place during the morning when some passengers managed to creep out of their cabins! The place became very noisy, like a holiday camp; the crew were trying to get everyone to join in, but not us!

We were two hours late getting in to Nassau owing to the rough weather, understanding there had been 20-foot-high waves!

Rosemary had made arrangements to meet friends on the island: a professor of the island's university and his wife Margaret. They lived at Delaporte, where boats could be seen coming in and out of the harbour from their flat. Margaret and her husband took us through the streets and then to the straw market, the famous part of the island, for souvenirs. We travelled to their home by bus. The seats down the aisle folded up to allow people up and down the bus. The vehicle looked ancient, more like a 1950s model and definitely not in first-class condition. The driver was happy-go-lucky, chatting to everyone. The police stopped the bus as the driver had let passengers off at an undesignated place, and he was fined 70 dollars.

Although the sea was very close to the flats, you had to be wary of sharks if you swam in the water, they came in so close to the shore.

Later in the day we had a tour of the island including an exclusive bay where famous people had houses, such as Elizabeth Taylor, Princess Margaret, Sean Connery and Julio Iglesias; small channels led up to their houses so that their boats could be moored close to home, as they were very expensive. A film crew were filming for a fashion magazine; as we stood watching they turned a Polaroid camera on to me, then gave me the shot!

The evening meal was with Rosemary's friends, in their home. While looking out of the window we saw hummingbirds drinking from their feeder. Our hosts started feeding them so that I was able to see them close up. They were fascinating, tiny birds that could hover; I will always remember them with the long beak.

We returned to the Red Boat for the night. As we walked back there was a steel calypso band on the promenade; really made you feel you were in the Caribbean.

On board there was a special 'midnight feast'. One of the chefs was carving a fish in ice; when he had finished it was perfect! He carved it in 20 minutes. One of these blocks of ice weighed 300 pounds. All types of food had been prepared and beautifully displayed; they also tasted very good even late at night. It appeared the majority of people spent most of their time eating, and what was served was sufficient for two of us! We remained in dock as it was to be very rough out in the open sea, so we had a good comfortable night's sleep.

On our rising the following morning, it was announced we would have an extra morning ashore, to allow the sea to calm before we left Nassau. We enjoyed the extra time as it was possible to see more of the locality. We returned to the boat for lunch, went on deck and watched the departure; the weather was beautiful. Once again the crew organised games around the swimming pool, but as it was so noisy we went inside. We decided that the Americans liked to be seen and heard!

When dark we went on the captain's deck and lay flat on deck chairs to look at the stars. The sky was very clear, but the Lad talking about star watching knew so little it was not worth being there. The sea was very smooth and no lights anywhere; the temperature was 21°C. We had been informed it was going to be yet another rough night; we actually decided to go to bed at 11.30pm, and true to form it was indeed once again a rough night.

I had vivid dreams of storms at home! Rosemary said I was talking in my sleep and making funny noises!

Next morning we rose early as we were to dock at 7am. Immigration came on board and we collected our passports. An announcement was made over the megaphone stating it would be three hours before we were allowed ashore. It had not been possible to land on the Bahamas as it was too rough to get in close. Would I go on a cruise again? No thank you!

This time a hotel had been booked at Cocoa Beach. We rested sitting by the side of the swimming pool, watching little lizards scuttle around us. They were about four or five inches long, quite harmless, and they just loved the sun. If you went near them they moved like lightning! The soil was very sandy and the water table high; if you dig down two feet in Florida you will strike water. This area was prone to short heavy showers and the worst area for thunderstorms. More people were killed by lightning here than anywhere else in America.

A taxi took us to a shopping area on Merritt Island, like some of the English malls. Being shrewd we watched for shops with sales and eventually purchased some silk clothes. The reason for being cheap was that they were not the 'in' colours; who worries?

The restaurant where we had the evening meal only sold steaks, but they were not true steaks but minced meat, so we were a little disappointed we had to eat them!

The next day was the last in America, so was spent preparing for the long journey home. There was plenty of rain and thunderstorms. The journey next day was an hour-long drive to the airport. Our driver explained that 308,000 acres of swamp land had been purchased by the state to be kept as a nature reserve. Early mornings it was not unusual to see alligators on the road, trying to get warm on the concrete until the traffic built up; he had also seen wild boar. A certain amount of poaching alligators occurred in the area; a medium-sized creature would bring in £1500 and this would be just for the skin. No one is supposed to feed alligators as this makes them spiteful and dangerous and they will attack people. There were poisonous snakes in the swamps and very few people attempted to go in there. Some remains had been found of people who had gone in and never returned after being killed by the snake bite.

The drive was very interesting with many little snippets of information. The flight for Manchester was late leaving and took seven and a half hours, travelling at 33,000 feet and up to 650 miles an hour. The tour was very interesting but I have no longing to return to that area; I would prefer another part of America.

Singapore, Australia and New Zealand
September to October 1996
(six weeks)

The holiday planning countdown had hit zero! Hours had been spent discussing where to go, what to see, and how long we should spend in various places including the complete time we should be away. Many problems had to be solved including illness and timetables to fit in, besides arrangements for the birds and animals at home to be looked after, but now we were setting off. The taxi arrived at 6.30am despite having been booked for 6.30pm, but all went well in the end, as it returned at the correct time for the airport.

After an hour and a half we arrived at Heathrow; we would have the usual wait after booking in, of two and a half hours before take-off. Long queues had formed at the four check-in desks. A first-class desk was opened for us owing to the long queues, luggage was dumped at the correct place and tickets collected with our seat numbers for the flight. Not first-class numbers; I wonder why? We had economy tickets!

We had been told that refreshments were to be served on the plane, but nothing about a full meal, so we ate in the restaurant before boarding the flight, only to find an hour later a full meal was served; this we had to let pass us by! As usual on the long flights, sleeping was almost impossible although we were travelling through the equivalent of the English night. The 13 hours took us over Amsterdam, close to Moscow, and then, avoiding trouble spots where war was in progress, over north-east India and along the coast of Burma, hence a slight detour.

On landing in the evening in Singapore (owing to time difference) we collected our luggage and, after a swift walk through customs, we were collected by a Quantas minibus to take us through the busy traffic. Our hotel being on the other side of the main city gave us the opportunity of a sightseeing tour on the way; the streets, shops and tall buildings were brightly lit. The hotel was situated in a quiet area that was better for sleeping. On arrival, although tired, we visited one of the two restaurants for some soup, delicious ice cream and coffee, and so to bed, no rocking required!

The next morning breakfast was served in Dennis's room on his balcony; this was an internal view and overlooked the second restaurant, which served seafood only. We had a continental breakfast which was brought to us. After this we started to find our way round the hotel, as it was quite large, and also the immediate vicinity outside, looking at the garden, the plants and the shrubs. The plants were eight or ten feet tall, while back in England they were kept in pots and never seemed to grow more the two feet high, all owing to the climate. The drains needed avoiding as the heat gave them a distinctive smell.

When going out we mostly went by taxi, and when one was requested at the hotel it soon arrived. The hotel had a light at the entrance and when it was put on any empty cabs would stop to pick up passengers. It was best to settle the price of the fare before getting in. Then we were taken down to the shops, but left outside the most expensive shops in Orchard Road; this is typical in most eastern countries. Taxis and minibuses all seem to be trained to do this, probably benefiting financially. This area is similar to Oxford Street in London. Being predictable tourists, it was not long before we walked on and found a much cheaper plaza in the next street. The Lucky Plaza fitted our pockets much better, although having been to Singapore once before I decided that prices had risen since then. The plaza had a variety of shops. Camcorders on offer were genuine and more advanced than those on sale in England. You still had to watch what you bought, as some goods were made especially for the tourist and were very poor quality. Enquiries were made and prices dropped; each time we walked away from the counters, extra items were then added.

The Fortune Plaza was the next stop, several minutes' walk away at the further end of the street. The ground floor of the building contained cafés of various descriptions, all selling eastern-style food. The smell reminded me of my visit to Hong Kong a few years prior. It was a relief to move away as the aromas were very pungent, but not before a gentleman came up the escalator with the remains of lunch on a plate. This was spilt down Dennis's trousers. Dennis showed his disapproval strongly, and eventually was paid to have them cleaned, but for the remainder of the day, he just smelt very strongly of the food!

Another large plaza only sold electrical goods and computers, plus everything that went with them. Laptop computers were popular but not worth purchasing to take home.

It was mid-afternoon before we returned to the hotel; the temperature and humidity had risen and we felt it as we tried to walk, so in to rest our weary bones!

Later we decided to visit the camcorder shop in the Lucky Plaza. This time we were offered a good price if I gave the camcorder I had in part exchange. Mine was already four years old, and also another £20 could be collected as a tax rebate on leaving the country with a new one. We splashed out and bought one each, knowing they were much more expensive back in England.

The evening meal we had back at the hotel; it was better to be careful where we ate owing to the lack of cleanliness at some places, locals were so used to the local bugs! Our dinner was a buffet consisting of a selection of cooked food in various heated dishes. Diners were invited to help themselves to anything, and as much as one liked. There were portions of duck, chicken, pork, more than one type of mushroom, potato balls, green beans, rice, chilli, a sprat-like fish, snapper, crab cooked in cabbage leaves, half a crab and many spicy sauces. This was the main course, then a further table contained noodles, croutons and coconut porridge. The porridge I particularly liked as it was sweet, contained whole rice and was served with cream on top. One of the tables had cakes, but nothing like those in England; there was no flour in them, and they were sweet and sticky. A coconut jelly contained peanuts. The head waiter, knowing we were trying various dishes, brought us plates with caramel pudding and fresh fruit. The fruits were from the island and so, being fresh, tasted much better than they would have having travelled to England.

As we were the last people dining that evening the head waiter came and talked and laughed with us. He was quite rotund and had a very infectious laugh and happy-go-lucky attitude. He told us about breakfast next day, then, remembering the video cameras we'd bought earlier, we retired to play with our new toys!

The second day opened with breakfast down in the restaurant; there was a choice of cooked or continental food, a good selection regardless of what was chosen. The cooked type of meal contained spicy soup, which had meat (I had no clue if it contained pork, beef or any other type of meat); there were also two or three varieties of rice with herbs, meat and scrambled eggs. They also tried to make an English type of breakfast, with bacon and fried eggs, but somehow it did not taste the same; I think this was because the curing of bacon was done quite differently.

Croissants and bread were available for the continental breakfast, alongside jam, marmalade or honey; wraps of butter were kept cool while floating in water and ice. Danish pastries were newly baked, and ice cubes floated like flotsam in fresh fruit juice. The real fruit juices were really superb; these I so enjoyed.

Using our camcorders was a novelty, so we went round the outside of the hotel, with the gardens and entrance. The humidity was high, hence the temperature appeared higher than registered; perspiration poured from us! There were open drains near the hotel boundaries, and these were definitely something to be avoided; they could be smelt before getting anywhere near them.

We made another short visit to the Lucky Plaza, where we purchased a remote control for the camcorders; the shop assistant dropped the price by the equivalent of £15 in English money before it was bought. The normal saying was 'You are my first customer today so a special price for you', as long as it was before midday! We thought they must have had a poor morning if that was so! It pays to barter with the locals; it is also something they expect from tourists, and it can be guaranteed they will drop a third of the price.

As taxis are the easiest method of transport and one of the cheapest, we used them most of the time to take us around; the next one took us from the plaza to Jurong Bird Park. The driver we engaged was very helpful and gave us a guided tour to the park, telling us all the important places as we passed. One thing the drivers said as soon as you entered the taxi, besides the destination, was 'You go football?' The men seemed football crazy, particularly watching English games. They knew all the famous names of players and for which club they played; we were astounded our English clubs were so popular. Manchester United and Liverpool were the most common clubs mentioned. It seemed difficult for them to believe we lived so far away from the grounds. This we presumed was because Singapore is such a small island compared to England. One or two drivers had travelled as far as London.

Jurong Park was in a delightful setting, masses of natural tall trees and shrubs, not to mention various colourful flower beds. Water was laid direct to the flower beds and automatically turned on over a given period of time. As usual we paid to enter. One thing that impressed us most was the number of free flying birds inside the park. It was difficult at first glance to tell which were native or captive. When we entered there were different species of macaws feeding together, including the hyacinth, a blue macaw. There are more of these in captivity than in the wild. The shoebill, which looked prehistoric, had an enormous beak and stood like a statue, with only the occasional blink of an eye that made you realise he was actually alive.

A large covered area was used to entertain people in comfort with demonstrations of the birds' abilities in flying, catching food and talking; also some unusual tricks had been learnt. A sulphur-crested cockatoo had been trained to take paper money from people in the audience; the money was returned later in the show. An Amazon parrot talked quite clearly and was ready for the titbit that followed.

In the park there was a section for birds of the cockatoo family; they were in an enormous flight, which contained some large trees. The trees had been damaged by the birds, so they did not require trimming by humans! Many birds were tame, but even so you had to realise how they could use their sharp beaks; they were strong enough to take your finger off! We spent a long time watching the birds in this cage, as there were so many different types. In adjoining flights there were birds from the tropical area; water was automatically turned on in given intervals to spray them; they enjoyed cooling down in the showers.

Moving on to a large lake we could see many water birds; pelicans were fun as they shovelled up fish from the lake. Some islands had been made for the birds, as some species enjoy sitting in the sun preening themselves. We sat in the cool, under a shady tree, watching. Close by was a monorail which quietly and slowly moved by; it was better for us to walk as we could stop and look as we wanted. Souvenir shops were placed at prominent locations, but so were the drink stands, and fruit juices were on hand. As the temperature was slowly rising it was time to move back to the hotel, with air conditioning; the insects biting had been enough for one day!

Outside the park was a taxi rank; you had to take the first in line. Ours was a known company, 'Comfort', but the taxi was anything but comfortable! The vehicle was in bad repair, rattles, shakes and noise, but that was not all. Each time we pulled up at traffic lights the driver promptly went to sleep! It became frightening; when we saw what was happening, we decided to keep the driver talking as we travelled, as ending up in hospital was not on our schedule!

A lazy time was spent snoozing, reading, writing some postcards in the hotel. The evening meal was a buffet and we took only the food we enjoyed. Afterwards we took a lift up to the roof, which contained a large outdoor swimming pool; no dip this evening but just enjoying the evening panorama with lights in the streets.

Friday, September 13: not unlucky for us! It was another enjoyable day, although we did stop to pack. This time we paid a visit to the island of Sentosa. We had a taxi ride to the highest point, for a cable car trip across to the island. On the cable car we passed over some of the docks. They are extremely busy with cargo in and out the whole time, exporting to all parts of the world.

Sentosa had a large butterfly farm, all outside but with netting over the top. It also contained some rooms showing types and colours of different beetles; they were all dead and set up in special frames. The actual butterflies have the most beautiful colours.

On the island was a large house which had been turned into a museum with some of the local history of Singapore, a large proportion about the 1939–45 war. Most of this was of the later years with the signing of the treaties. There was a depiction of the signing with natural lifelike figures. I could recognise most of the figures from pictures I had seen in national papers etc. Of course in the museum the Burma Railway could not be forgotten. After spending a considerable amount of time in there, we caught the island bus down to the ferry, then returned to the mainland by water. We had hoped to visit Chinatown during the evening, but time rolled on.

6.15pm arrived too quickly and we had to return to the airport by taxi. While waiting for the taxi in the hotel, I talked to some people who were waiting to return to England. Through conversation we found they came from Pulborough where I was brought up. It so happened we both knew various people in the village. They knew the farm where we lived, the school I attended. Fancy travelling that distance to find someone like that; what a coincidence!

Regarding the taxi to the airport, the driver was very talkative so we gained a considerable amount of information. Some areas in Singapore were reserved for certain taxis; others infringing on the area had to pay penalties. The road tax for a taxi was the equivalent of £3,800 to keep the vehicle on the road for a year. He explained his home was a government-built flat; this was being paid off on a mortgage. Taxi fares here were not very high. Often taxis were in bad condition; certainly maintenance was required on several we had travelled in.

We were queuing for our flights to Sydney when I realised we had not paid the airport tax, so I had to dash to the bank to change some travellers cheques, just in time as Dennis had reached the checkout counter; the tax was taken as the luggage was pushed through.

It was not long before we boarded; the aircraft had arrived from Frankfurt, Germany. This flight took six hours 48 minutes (half the time from London to Singapore). Dennis managed a sleep but as usual I was wide awake. Dennis met a person from

Slovenia on the flight; she had lived in Melbourne for 42 years, but still had a strong accent. She proved a real character at the age of 72! She had a terrific sense of humour; we had many a laugh. She had been well educated and could discuss many subjects; in fact other than Dennis's sleep she kept us occupied most of the way. At last it was 'touchdown' at Sydney airport; we landed at 5.45am, a bright beautiful dawn, but chilly after Singapore temperatures of 32°C.

Part 2: Touring Australia

We felt rather jetlagged, in fact more than on a long flight! Ray Ackroyd and his wife Beryl met us at the airport and helped to carry the luggage to the car, where we piled in. We had booked a holiday with him to show us the bird and wildlife around Sydney. As it was so early he took us for a drive around the area, in the region of 20 miles. We saw the river where the Olympics were to be held, the following Australian summer. We passed a new housing estate, which showed the modern architecture; we also noticed there were many bungalows. Birds were now rising and beginning their morning songs, especially as it was spring in Australia.

Eventually the rooms were ready for us at the Warwick Farm hotel; we were introduced to the staff and went to our luxurious rooms that Ray had booked. I just curled up in bed and slept for some time after a shower. We left the hot and sticky weather behind. After waking Dennis joined me and we spent the time just looking out the window, and listening to any birds. The temperature was much more mellow with a slight breeze; it was very pleasant.

During the afternoon there was a wedding in the hall below us and out in the garden. The bride must have been nervous as she spent the time smoking. She was dressed in a cream-coloured dress; the three bridesmaids wore white tops with black skirts. Many guests brought gifts in a variety of boxes. After this we watched the feathered type of birds! There were fruit bats in the distance, which we saw through the binoculars as they started flying when it was getting dark.

The evening meal was at the hotel; we were too tired to go out and look round! We could hear the disco in the room adjoining the restaurant, so a noisy dinner. We ate potato and leek soup; I cannot remember the main dish, but the sweet was a pavlova with vanilla ice cream. After that it was to bed as we had an early start in the morning.

A good cooked breakfast started the day properly. Ray and Beryl, who were to be our guides for the coming eight days, arrived at the hotel. This was to be our special tour to see as much as possible of the Australian birds. Ray was known as the 'bird man of Australia'. We were not quite sure what to expect, except we had received some very friendly correspondence from them, fitting in the things we were particularly interested in. Our luggage was put in their trailer behind their Toyota Cruiser, a four-wheel drive; this was mainly for trips in the outback.

The first stop was after an hour's journey climbing into the Blue Mountains, a name that aptly describes them. The colour comes from the gas given off by the leaves of the eucalyptus, of which there are over 500 varieties. Certain species are common to different parts of Australia. Australia is a very large country and has a variance of climate. It takes nearly seven hours to fly from Sydney (east coast) to Perth (west coast). Just think: in England we are only two hours from Rome! Picnic tables and barbecues are set up everywhere, as the climate encourages this type of living, so many meals are eaten outside.

Many species of birds were seen in our short drive; we paused to film where there was a large group of sulphur-crested cockatoos, our first sight of them in the wild. Pennants, shrikes and magpies were seen flying. The magpies are not like the English breed; they have more black colouring. The currawongs look more like our magpies, but their song is nothing like any English bird. They appeared everywhere including in the towns.

We stopped to look at Wentworth Falls, although there was little water, as no rain had fallen lately. The Falls fell into a green valley below. Ray and I went for a walk to get a better view. It was wonderful to stop and admire even the common shrubs and trees of Australia. They are only ever seen in hot houses back home. There were different types of banksia, some in bloom and others with large seed pods which the black cockatoos love. As it was spring their wattle (our mimosa) was in full bloom, standing out amongst the dry grasses. Most of the trees retain their leaves during the winter months.

Next stop was Echo Valley, a very popular place for tourists, with coach areas for many Japanese visitors. They stop for ten minutes and push on to the next venue, but we were able to take our time and stop when we wanted! Ray and Beryl were so considerate. We had a picnic lunch. Beryl had so much food stored away in the trailer she amazed us at every meal time, and never the same each day; Ray had specially baked some cakes for us. We were having one such meal when a helicopter came over us and landed not far away. We learnt later a man had been climbing rocks at the edge of the valley, slipped and damaged his leg badly, so he had been taken to hospital.

A tourist shop at the top of the valley had been feeding the birds in the wild. The birds waited in the scrubland, close to the feeders. They were beautiful, having red feathers, with blue on their wings. At the base of the tree, some rats were also waiting to scrounge feed.

After this break we drove down into the valley where Ray was brought up as a child. The valley was not particularly wide but very long. Most of the houses were built 30 or 40 years ago, with the exception of one old house and buildings. Only the ribs and some wooden panels remained. This was one of the settlements in the area; you could visualise families growing up in the peace and quiet, with mountains surrounding the area. A stream ran along the side of the road; we could hear the croaking of the frogs; every pond or stream had some, but they were almost impossible to see. On the opposite side of the road were the remains of a disused railway junction; all types of iron machinery pertaining to the railway were still lying around rusty with age. There was no electricity, just steam engines with water. Rails were still on the track in places, with a dilapidated truck that had carried goods in the past. The railway station remained as a piece of rusty corrugated building practically falling apart; it makes one wonder what tales it could tell.

Now on to a small town called Blackheath; we had a look at the local shops, and to our surprise discovered that the largest was an antique shop. We found that a group of people ran the shop, each having their own antiques, many things we would think not worth saving, such as old tins and cracked vases from the early 1900s. There was a school desk and chairs of different styles, not forgetting other household furniture, which all needed repairing. Back in England they would have been designated to the tip. There was chinaware and some silver.

Ray drove us on to a garden with rhododendrons, but unfortunately they had not yet come into bloom.

At the Redleaf hotel we settled in for the night, joining Ray and Beryl for the evening meal. The meals were served by Australians, and were large, too big for the average British person. They ate enormous plates full of food, and cleared them! There was roast beef, roast potatoes, carrots, courgettes and broccoli; it would have been nicer if it had been cooked longer. This was the main fault of the Australians. The meal was completed with passion fruit and banana cheesecake. After this meal we had to have a walk round before thinking of bed. Postcards and daily notes were written for the day, before we fell into our respective beds.

September 16 and this was Beryl's birthday, just 21 again, like the rest of us! Dennis and I had breakfast together while Ray and Beryl loaded the trailer with luggage and food for the day. Not far was Govetts Leap, from where we would be able to photograph birds in that area. The place was named after a highwayman called Govett; he had stolen from people travelling and the police were after him. They cornered him at the last attempt and rather than be caught by them, he rode his horse over the steep hill in 1831. There was an enormous drop into the valley below, so both he and his horse died. There is a large statue depicting Govett and his horse in the village, and a memorial on the side of the hill where he jumped over the edge.

As we looked over the valley we could see the results of last year's very bad fires; they destroyed so many acres. Where the ground undulated the tops of the hills had the new growth of shrubs while the sides still had tall trees. The fires had swept the tops of the hills and left the remainder untouched. It was here we saw the gang-gang cockatoo, a beautiful grey bird with a red head and crest that curled towards the beak; we actually saw a pair.

Also there were rose robins and blue wrens. This was a haven for the birds, and we were here before the main day trippers arrived.

During the day we stopped and watched many birds of interest. Some of the ground was very rough with boulders; sheep grazed here but there appeared so little for them to eat. We stopped for lunch in the bush not far from a small pond, where frogs continually croaked. While Ray and Beryl collected the remains of the picnic, Dennis and I walked and found two kangaroo skeletons; Ray thought they were probably road casualties.

Along the road a citrus farm was for sale and to attract attention the owners had painted the fruit and made them red. It obviously caught our eye!

We had one stop which was a little disappointing at Hartley, where a convicts' jail was situated; it was supposed to be open every day, but when we arrived it was closed and no one was interested in our arrival. Ray said he would not be taking anyone else there. The convicts had been deported from England; they had helped to build this village, as well as the prison and the accommodation for the warders.

On the way to Bathurst we passed a car which had broken down, with two women looking helpless. Ray turned round and helped; the car was almost on fire, it was so hot! Ray telephoned the nearest garage but could do no more. We had coffee beside a large lake; this was used as a reservoir; as no rain had fallen of late it was rather low in water. A speedboat had been the whole length of the lake before returning to a spot beside us. The lunch was later and several miles from here; Beryl and Ray produced the table and chairs out in the bush, and yet again we had a lovely picnic with plenty of food; every day was different.

After this we travelled further and came across some wood ducks, with 12 ducklings, on a small pond beside the road. We next came to the gold mining village of Sofala; in 1851 it was a very large and profitable place due to the gold, with 25,000 people living there. The gold has since been worked out and only one or two people remain there living in hopes the river will bring some down to them. We saw a man panning but he had little results, enough to pay for a weekend there, but certainly not a fortune. There were still some old shacks standing in the village reminding people of the past. There was a shop that sold some small nuggets of gold, and opals. Dennis bought an opal pendant and found out later it was worth double what he had paid. A second shop was opposite, and had everything including the kitchen sink; it was packed from floor to ceiling but with mostly second-hand goods, such as Oxo, tobacco, baking tins and any other tins you'd like to think of, along with china, books and turntable music records.

The area was still hilly although we had left the mountains of Katoomba behind. The ground was very poor, but a small flock of sheep were wandering finding something to eat. It was only when we got near Lake Windermere the land was more fertile, but there was no sight of crops until we got near the small town of Mudgee. There were many vineyards here and it was known as 'Hunter Valley'; the wines from here were exported to England, and were well known.

The night was spent at the Soldier hotel at Mudgee. There was a serviceman's club opposite where we had the evening meal. Any serviceman's club provided a good inexpensive evening meal; this was only the first of many we visited in Australia. We went to bed at a reasonable time, but the night was not as restful as we had hoped!

I was woken at 11.15pm by the sound of gunshots: not a comfortable experience when alone in a strange room. Someone let off more shots, and the person in the room above started coughing violently. My first thought was he had been shot. Men were running around, so I lay still and kept quiet, not even looking out of the window; I was afraid someone was drunk and firing at anything that moved. Not long after this I heard men's voices, cars arriving; obviously it was a policeman shouting for the guest above to open the door and come out; they were then told to lie on the floor and put their hands behind them. After some time all went quiet and the cars drove away.

It was the next day when I heard the full story. One of the Australian cattle product firms had a group of salesmen staying at the hotel; there were six of them. They had got drunk and decided to play a prank on the guests staying in the hotel. The coughing was not someone hurt, but he was laughing so much it made him cough. The owner of the hotel heard the shots and came out to see what was happening. By then Dennis had left his room and carefully climbed the stairs to the next floor; he saw people running from one room to another and laughing; he was able to tell the owner which rooms were involved. When the police arrived they went straight to the rooms concerned and made the one with the gun lie on the floor while the room was searched. The police eventually allowed the men to stay after their explanations were given. While all this was happening, two men came out of the club opposite, only to hear gunshots; one of them collapsed with a heart attack, the second man ran to the police to get them to send for an ambulance and take his friend to hospital!

After breakfast next morning, the men came down as though nothing had happened. Dennis said to them, 'I hope you enjoyed your childish pranks'! Ray, our guide, telephoned the headquarters of the firm for which the men worked, and complained very strongly. Later in the day we heard that all the men involved in the prank had been given notice and so they lost their jobs! The men were in their late thirties so should have known better. So ended our excitement – or was it so exciting? I think not!

We left Mudgee with memories that would remain with us; the land was no longer rough bushland, but grass where many sheep grazed, with some arable crops. A group of corn silos were seen; these could hold a large tonnage of corn. Ray drove to the highest point so that we had a good view of the area. While up there we had our first sighting of wild kangeroos. They came towards us, so Beryl and Dennis made their way down the field hoping to get a closer look.

Gulagong was not so many miles from Mudgee and still in the farming area. It was here we visited an agriculture museum. Many farm implements were on display, tools that I had seen in use in my younger days, on the farm or in houses, or had disposed of when they got into a bad state. There were paraffin lamps, all sizes and shapes, and tools we had forgotten about. Information was available on various regiments that served in the 1939–45 war. Australia played a large part in the Asian area; uniforms, badges, medals and maps were on show. Dennis and I spent some time looking round.

We then drove on to Dunedoo, stopping for coffee and to watch some birds; there were hundreds of sulphur-crested cockatoos and galahs on either side of the road. One barn contained implements, straw and obviously some corn. The birds appeared to be picking up a large amount of food. It was along this road Ray showed us how to see birds that were nesting. He would spot a likely nesting hole and tap on the trunk of the tree, and a head would appear out of the hole, before the bird would fly off. If you waited quietly it was not long before the bird returned. Ray did this many times, showing different species of birds nesting.

In the village we spent time looking round several antique shops before going on to see more nesting birds. The narrow lanes were lined with trees and a likely location for us to find nesting birds. Most of the trees were gum trees, so it was easy to see the holes; the nests were approximately 10 or 12 feet above ground. As it was spring there were many nesting birds. The temperature was pleasant and warm; cardigans were left in the vehicle, but midges found our arms instead!

There was a row of peppercorn trees where we sheltered out of the sun to have a cup of coffee. The trees could have been oak trees as they were a similar shape and had little seeds intermingled with the leaves. Red-rumped parrots fed on the ground close to us; they were not easy to distinguish as the greens of their feathers were the same as the grass. We moved further on the tour on an unmade road; this is not unusual in Australia! It was here we caught up with a flock of sheep being moved. There were four men, five dogs and 2000 sheep. Ray and I got out and spoke to the men and also helped drive the flock for about a mile. It was so interesting talking to the men. Beryl drove the vehicle following us.

For the night we stopped at a private guest house; we had bed, breakfast, and an evening meal. Beryl said she had stayed there many times. They were very pleasant people, making us very welcome with Australian home cooking. The house was close to the river so in the early morning I enjoyed a walk along the banks; it had turned colder overnight so I wore a jacket.

Ray filled the 'Cruiser' with diesel next morning and left us to browse around a large store in the village, where we found more film for the camera, and some oddments. It was interesting comparing prices with those at home. When we moved off we saw more birds and nests en route to a large farm. The farmer had two plots of 150 acres of bearded wheat, a field of 100 acres of oats, and another 100 acres of barley. He had a suckled shorthorn herd in one field; in the other field were ostriches, which had in the past been used for meat production. Now only six remained; there was insufficient money in breeding them.

The main reason to visit the farm was to see the farmer's hobby. He had built many aviaries and in particular two very large flights, with an open barn but covered. The flights were approximately 50 feet long, 30 feet wide and 20 feet high. The birds had the freedom to fly in this area. We went inside the first one; it contained a selection of species, which the farmer said was to prove that birds could all live together and breed. It was delightful to see the pairs. Some were already nesting in boxes provided, and others thinking about it; it was only when another bird flew too close that they showed their disapproval. There were Major Mitchells, sulphur-crested cockatoos, bare-eyed corellas, red-tailed black cockatoos, Alexandrines, Barrabands, Pennants, galahs and bluebonnets, and so a good mixture of species.

The second large flight also had many birds, but these were tamer and just loved being handled. They came and settled on my shoulder, also on my camera or on my head. It was lovely; we could have stayed there all day. A corella spent some time climbing over me, full of mischief. Outside the larger flights the farmer had some small flights with small birds; these were in pairs for breeding. There were red-rumps, sun conures and ringnecks. Even these were very tame. There were some fancy pheasants, in large runs, and special flights for macaws. Not many people knew about these birds as certain people in Australia were keen to steal and sell for money. Ray had been bird-watching with the farmer.

Also on the farm were chickens, and free-range kangaroos that had been injured by cars, plus an albino which would have died in the wild. This was a novelty for visitors. The kangaroos were tame as we fed them with bread. Amongst the farmer's collection was a magpie goose; it was picked up after being found injured in the northern territory and now followed him like a dog, either walking round or, when he was driving the pickup, flying beside the vehicle or on the roof.

Top: kangaroos waiting for titbits. Bottom: wild birds being fed.

After the enjoyable morning we were taken back through Dubbo and then in a southerly direction on minor roads to a nature reserve by a river at Jincilla. By now it was very hot so it was pleasant to sit in the shade for our lunch. Beryl could still always find something different for our lunch; this time it was salad and silverside beef, salmon, cheese and biscuits, pure orange juice to drink and more fresh fruit to eat.

A subject not normally mentioned: the ladies' toilets. A wooden building away from the picnic area, but there were no doors or water. Beryl and I laughed and wondered how many other people had done the same.

The Abercrombie River had little water as it had been some time since the rains. The bridge was made of large trees, but I could well imagine when there was heavy rain the bridge would be washed away! There were two families camping with cars, a lorry and a tent, ferrets and two Jack Russell dogs. They were wandering around living on what they could find. They told us about catching rabbits with dogs and ferrets. They were almost like English hippies just moving around the countryside. They appeared very happy with fewer worries than some; perhaps they had the right idea!

Not long after leaving here we were able to see a kookaburra, sitting on a fence post close to the road. Nearby was scrubland with large holes; Ray explained that they were made by eastern wombats. The animals were mostly nocturnal and the size of a suckling pig. There was a second type called the 'hairy-nosed wombat', but these were mostly in the northern area of Australia. Farmers called the wombats pests; although not officially vermin, many were shot as they did so much damage to the ground and crops with their burrowing.

We arrived at Oberon late afternoon after watching for nests on the way. At the end of this journey we had covered about 300 kilometres, the longest journey on the tour. Dennis felt very tired. The accommodation was at the Trout Motel. The sign outside was of a large trout jumping into the water. The 'cut out' trout was about five metres long. It was painted in natural colours. We had our meal at the restaurant opposite our rooms. It poured with rain the whole evening, the first we had seen. The food was piled onto our plates; I think they thought we ate like the Aussies! I had a mixed grill – pork and lamb chops, sausages, steak, mushrooms, onions, peas and chips. We saw some plates of food like it just disappear in no time. It was not possible to leave the table feeling hungry.

After Ray and Beryl unloaded the trailer they found the water had seeped into Beryl's and Dennis's cases. Most of the clothes had to be dried overnight.

Thursday, a beautiful morning after the heavy night's rain; everywhere smelt fresh. Breakfast was served to us in our rooms, once again too much on our plate. We had to waste food rather than have an uncomfortable journey; at least that was my excuse! Beryl had been ill during the night; I had indigestion so it kept me awake. Everything was packed and returned to the trailer. Ray had put another tarpaulin over the trailer in case of more rain.

The journey to the national park was over dusty unmade winding roads, up over hills, down into the valleys and up again, with hairpin bends. We eventually arrived in a valley which was very green. It was here we saw the bower bird, a lovely sheen on its feathers, showing dark mauves and blues. The female was less colourful with dirty green plumage and a speckled breast, but suitable for camouflage. The male bird does not mature for six years, and starts with the same coloured feathers as the female. Ray found a nest where the male picks up coloured stones and objects, particularly the colour blue, then shapes the grasses into a crescent over the objects. He will entice his wife there but if she does not like it she walks away and he has to start again, until she thinks it is suitable.

It was also in this park that we saw king parrots; they came close as we fed them while having our lunch. As usual Beryl had laid out a lovely picnic with yet different types of food. She really did us proud.

We drove back along the winding road, where we could see vehicles had gone over the edge with sheer drops into the valley below. It was difficult to pass another vehicle owing to the narrow road and unmade surface. Rock formations were unusual and looked like the top of a castle where the erosion had caused this formation. Lower down we found wild banana plants in flower, and many other species, blooming.

A famous tunnel in the rock convicts had dug out by hand; there was no machinery in those days. It was several feet wide and long; we were able to drive through. Later we saw our first yellow-tailed black cockatoo, eating nuts in a tree at the side of the road. The ground was strewn with the remains of pine cones; this was a sure sign they were busy.

Yass was the next stop for the night. It had been threatening to rain all day but remained fine until we had eaten the evening meal, when a thunderstorm broke overhead. For the evening meal Dennis was able to have his 'bugs', a type of crawfish. I had camembert cheese fried in wedges and served with large king prawns, followed by a banana split. We all had an early night to bed; another storm and showers woke us during the night.

A wet morning followed, not a very encouraging start as over an inch of rain had already fallen. This was needed by the farmers as the ground was so dry; it had not rained for months in this area. We visited the Highland mountains; there were more zigzagging roads, but there was tarmac on the roads. Our road took us into another valley near a reservoir. There was more water in the reservoir than in Sydney Harbour, so we were told. The lake was 50 kilometres long and between four and five wide!

This was another nature reserve called Burrinjuck, and although it was still raining Beryl and Ray put on rain jackets and fed the birds to show how tame they were. How many English guides would have done the same so we could see the native birds? This was a popular area for the public to come to feed the birds. They were very tame, landing on people's heads and hands.

We decided to have coffee and while we did so it stopped raining. So now it was our turn to feed the birds; they landed on our heads, shoulders and hands. At one time I had approximately the value of £2000 or £3000 resting and feeding on me. Dennis said this was the happiest day of his life. After returning home I copied a photograph, sewing in cross-stitch this day with him covered in the wild parrots. There were so many different species of parrots and other birds flying around waiting for some food.

As we walked across the park there were wild kangaroos coming to be fed. It was so interesting to see the baby 'joeys' in the pouches; some took food out of their parent's mouth although inside the pouch, their long legs hanging out as there was no room to place them inside. This was a real haven for all wildlife. I stood and filmed a blue wren; they have longer tails than the English wren and also hold theirs high behind them. As it was a damp morning we enjoyed our own company instead of many other visitors. Ray and Beryl more or less had to drag us away. On the way out we came to a waterfall; it was on one side of the road, then it ran under the road and down a slope into a valley.

Back to Yass again when Beryl visited one of her favourite pie shops for our lunch. By now the temperature had dropped from 28°C to 11°C; this we really felt. Now on for another 80 kilometres to Berrima. There were several antique shops, but all rubbish. From here we went to Balaclava, Boirla and Moss Vale. After this circular drive, we returned to the Bakers House, where we stayed the night; it had at one time been a bakery. They only served breakfast here so we went down the road to another hotel for a meal. This was more like an English pub. You bought your own meat there and cooked it on a barbecue which was provided. Ray cooked the steak and we helped ourselves to the various salads and vegetables. In another room was a folk group playing their instruments and singing. Some of the singers sounded as though they had had more than a glass or two! We returned to our own hotel and made coffee and talked about the day.

I rose extra early next morning as I had agreed to meet Ray to go on an early bird watch. The others slept on! So many birds were up and feeding. On our way we passed the local prison, where inmates worked in the garden. Ray said he had spoken to one of the prisoners, who had been a judge in the courts; he had obviously been in trouble, and had now lost his job. We filmed the yellow-tailed cockatoos who were feeding on seeds in the trees; where some of the seeds had fallen, others were eating them on the ground. The females had white beaks, while the males had black beaks; it was easy to differentiate between the two. By the time we returned to the motel breakfast could be smelt as it cooked.

At 9am, everything had been repacked and we were on our way to Morton Park and Fitzroy Falls. As we pulled in to the park, a Pennant sat at the entrance to its nest, but stayed long enough for us to photograph.

In the car park near the waterfall we found a lyrebird scratching in the scrub for worms; this was a female so did not display much of a tail. The birds are great mimics. Ray and I walked round to get a better view of the falls. There was only a trickle of water as there had not been any rain. Dennis tried to find some of the croaking frogs but they were too well hidden. This was a nature reserve so it had the usual souvenir shop! This was one way of helping to support the reserve financially.

We had a quiet drive through Kangaroo Valley, a delightful lush area, but very frosty in winter. This part of Australia was an appealing place to live, not many houses and not too close together. Very few houses are built in Australia; the living accommodation is mostly bungalows and they are built on stilts to keep the termites out.

Hampton Bridge was in the lower part of the valley, with three shops close by; these were primarily for tourists. One was very picturesque with highly scented jasmine along the veranda and around the door. Inside was a plethora of gifts, such as local pottery; these were interesting figures, not only standing but made to sit on the edge of the shelves. China of many designs was on display, silver jewellery which was handmade, jams, chutneys and any amount of knick-knacks.

At the entrance and exit to the bridge was a parapet in a castle style and a plaque stating that convicts had built the bridge in 1898. These men had been sent from England for stealing sheep and possibly disobeying the law in other ways. Most of the men were made to work like slaves in the hot climatic conditions and for very little food. This bridge is a big attraction as it is not far from Sydney.

Kiama, our next stop, was still a few miles away as we travelled north. The nearer we got to Sydney the better the roads were, both width and surface, but unfortunately there was more traffic. Kiama is on the east coast and 80 miles from Sydney. Our motel overlooked a bay, a real surfing area. The sea was such a deep blue and had large rolling waves. Ray took us on a quick tour of the area, walking round the lighthouse to see the famous 'blow hole'. When it was almost high tide water blew between some rocks rather like a whale releasing air through its blow hole!

After a coffee we went to a village called Berry; on the way back we found 'Six Mile Beach'. There were miles of sand and no one about. On the road inland there were several dairy herds where herds were penned in for milking.

The day had been cold, so we put on something warmer before crossing the road to a hotel for dinner. This particular evening was the last we spent with Ray and Beryl, so they spent more than usual on the meal. I had veal, Dennis had barramundi fish and we all had a glass of wine. Our waiter took photographs on Beryl's camera. An electronic piano played pleasant tunes during the meal. An evening with happy memories! We all retired to bed before 10pm.

An early morning walk at 7am had been planned with Ray. It was chilly; a jacket was required. The idea was to see the fishermen come in with their catch of fish; unfortunately the tide was wrong so they had not been fishing! Dennis and I had breakfast together and as usual discussed the previous day's events. This was our last day with Ray and Beryl.

The trailer was packed with all the luggage, photographs taken. A last hot cup of coffee; this time we sat in a garden with flower beds. As usual Ray found a hole in a tree trunk, but no one was at home! We went back to Kiama for a fish and chip lunch on the quay. Some small fishing boats had come in. Sitting outside on the picnic benches we ate lunch with gulls trying to help themselves and pelicans standing and hoping! Later Ray and Beryl took us to the hotel near the airport at Sydney, where we would stop to look at Sydney for the next few days.

Ray and Beryl had made this tour one never to be forgotten!

Part 3: Australia Alone

We were now on our own for the remainder of the holiday. After looking at the price of meals at the hotel we walked on and found a rowing club, which was nearby. Here it was only $6 for the two meals, one each. The orange drink was almost as much at $2 per glass. Beryl had told us to keep an eye out for these clubs. After the meal we walked back to the hotel.

For breakfast next morning there was a large selection to choose from, either continental or cooked. One thing we noticed was that cooked tomatoes always had cheese on the top, even for breakfast.

We were disappointed with the hotel; the money and the rooms did not match. Conditions did not come up to standard, stains on the carpets, bedspreads felt dirty. The booking had been for two nights but we decided to look elsewhere, for a cleaner environment and more reasonable price, for the following night. We had been in contact for another place but this was worse!

We had a walk round to a bank and then to Darling Harbour. It was unrecognisable compared with 1992; many new buildings had been built on the northern side of the harbour; there was a shopping complex which included a conference centre, restaurants and miles of pavements. Ice creams of many flavours were on offer costing the equivalent of £3 each, and a cup of coffee for £1.10. As our feet tired we took a ride on the pavement train; this took us to the other side of the harbour, close to the aquarium and booking office for the ferry. The sulphur-crested cockatoo was still outside the office as he had been four years prior. He entertained the passing visitors. There was a monorail that took 15 minutes to cover the circuit around part of Sydney and cost $2.50 (£1.50). A ferry at the quay would take passengers to the Circular Quay; this saved a lot of walking. The old wharfs were still there and were in the process of being repaired and painted, and being used for business projects.

Enquiries were made at the tourist bureau regarding another hotel for us to stay the night, but other than passing us a brochure they were not interested. We also found the hotel we stayed at was no longer a 'flag hotel'; it had been downgraded, although it still said in the bedrooms that it was a flag hotel. We had to stay there another night after all, so we went to the rowing club for dinner and Dennis won £35 on the lottery. After returning to the hotel we discussed finding another hotel for the following night.

A lazy beginning to the next day, as Dennis did not believe in early rising! After breakfast we signed out; we had a considerable discussion at reception over the hotel not being a flag hotel, but were unable to get the bill reduced. Enquiries were made regarding the hotel we stayed at in 1992, but we were unlucky as it had changed hands and certainly looked in poor condition. Not far from Potts Point was a De Vere hotel. The receptionist apologised profusely as the builders were in and no food could be provided. This did not worry us as I had been in this locality before and knew of a good restaurant close by. Dennis unfortunately left one of his bags on the bus when we moved to the new hotel. Luckily the bus company were good and delivered it on the next bus to the De Vere hotel, so all was well.

When I came to pay my Mastercard was not accepted, so I had to make a telephone call to London to find out why: rather embarrassing! All was solved later in the day. The temperature was rising as the day progressed to 32°C, no cardigans or pullovers required. We heard the call of a parrot in the main street; through watching we found a sulphur-crested cockatoo had a nest in the guttering on top of a tall building.

The following day we went to the botanical gardens, which were within walking distance, and three hours were spent there. Although it was early spring many trees and shrubs were in bloom. One tree had blooms on the trunk. Ducklings had been hatched; we watched them swim in a drain and then disappear into the open sea; the waves were quite large for the little birds and they looked like corks bobbing around, but they survived. It had been a tiring but interesting day.

It was breakfast a la Paris, outside under umbrellas at our favourite restaurant, where we watched the unusual fountain; it looked like the seed head of a dandelion. We browsed in many shops but did not buy anything as the money had to last us a few more weeks. Close to these shops a seaman had constructed two miniature sailing ships from wood. They were approximately two feet long. He had spent many hours perfecting all the details. People admired his work and he had a box for donations to help children in Asia. We then took the time to stand (or sit) and stare; it is certainly something we have little time to do. People of many colours and sizes walked by, and not one did we know!

September 27: the day we had to say goodbye to Sydney, travelling to the airport by the special bus. We had booked the flight to Brisbane; although it was an internal flight we had to book in an hour before take-off. We watched aircraft come in and out before ours came in. It was late as the international part of the airport was extremely busy; a slot had to be found for us to fly out. It was the children's two-week holiday in New South Wales. The size of Australia being so big, the flight gave us time to have lunch and snooze before arriving. We had booked a hire care in advance; it was waiting for us at the airport. The motel was on the northern side and a map helped us navigate; according to the driver, I was not good at navigating, but somehow we arrived!

It was a pleasant quiet motel; our rooms were at the back, which was even quieter! The evening meal was enjoyed and we gleaned more information for the following day. The manager advised us not to drive into the city as parking was very difficult.

Unfortunately Dennis was not well next morning so he stayed in bed while I walked around the area. Later in the day we took a chance and drove down to the river and market area. There was a butterfly area like Sentosa in Singapore, so we did not spend money to go in. A small band was playing and marching in and out of the flower gardens and around the market. The stalls were interesting to look at as many tourist gifts were on show. Many dried flower arrangements around pictures and wall decorations. This drew my attention to the various flowers and grasses. I bought a pair of earrings made to look like galahs. It was really more interesting looking than buying.

One thing that distracted Dennis from the market was a building which advertised birds and animals. He just could not pass it by! We went in and found that numerous species that were native to Australia were kept in a very large aviary, more the size of an English barn. Instead of a solid roof it was covered with strong wire netting. If it rained the birds got wet. There was a rosella that decided it did not like me, and attacked every time it flew by me! I got wise to this and ducked to one side as it decided to have another try. Dennis and other visitors enjoyed a laugh. This particular parrot was an exception as other birds had been hand-reared, and we handled a kookaburra. The keepers handled opossums, lizards and scorpions and invited us to touch them. One girl held a baby wombat; it had a very rough coat. The koalas were sleepy as they are nocturnal, but also the eucalyptus leaves they eat act like a drug and make them sleepy. After spending a long time in there we went out for a snack lunch close to the river.

Dennis could not forget the birds so we went in for the second time. The colours of the birds were not startling, it was just the behaviours that were so fascinating. One of the hand-reared flying foxes, which we had not seen the first time, came to the footpath. Someone had given it a piece of apple to eat, so it was possible to touch the bat. It had soft rusty-coloured fur, with a fox-like face, but large teeth, which it decided to use if your hand was in the wrong place! When hanging on a branch it was about eight inches long; it was quite an experience to have one so close. Everything was so interesting in there with the birds and animals.

The evening was lazy just watching television, *The Bill* and *Heartbeat*. Later on the tour we saw other English programmes.

It was 10am when we left the motel, with the luggage reloaded. Soon we were on the Bruce Highway, the main road to the north of Australia, as we were driving to Cairns, which was nearly 1000 miles away. The scenery was varied, but we did not photograph as it rained most of the day. We were unlucky; rain had not fallen for months, so locals were pleased to see it. We passed pine forests that belonged to the government. Lookouts were placed throughout the forest to check against fire. Fire risk was always very high. Some of the hills were a pyramid shape;

the highest points were pointed. The plains had scrubland, where some cattle grazed, but the ground looked so barren. Each farm probably contained thousands of acres.

Nearer to Bundaberg the land was better quality, with grazing much better. The soil colour had changed and was now red; not far away the soil was black.

Lunch was purchased from a supermarket in Gympie, where bread roll, cheese and fruit made a sufficient snack. We could not buy much at a time as there was nowhere to store it, except the boot of the car; as temperatures rose the boot became steadily hotter. We did carry some powdered soup and a flask of hot water, making a change as well as nourishing.

We had now started to drive into the sugar cane area; there were fields of it in various stages of growth, from planting to harvesting. The Reef Gateway Motel in Bundaberg we made the stopover for the night. There was shelter for the car under a corrugated roof, just outside our rooms. Before going to bed we visited a small village called Bargara; the wind was quite strong although no rain at the time. I remained in the car as the wind was too strong for me: not favourite coastal weather for me! We were hoping to see Fraser Island and found when we got back it was over 20 miles from us. Tours were run into Hervey Bay, which was between the island and us, to see the humpback whales, possibly the following day. The whales come from the Antarctic to give birth to their calves in September.

The restaurant at the motel was closed as it was Sunday, so down the road we went to a 'Sizzler', which was one of a chain of restaurants, like the English roadside cafés. As we were pensioners we were offered a special rate and a drink. It was possible to eat as much as we liked, with a side salad, steak, baked potatoes and also a selection of sweets, plus coffee. For the two of us it cost £10.

As usual I wrote up notes every day, covering anything I thought would be interesting. It started to rain really hard; you could hear people say how nice it was to have the rain; needless to say we were not so keen, especially as there was a forecast of more rain the following day.

Breakfast was at 7.45am. There was a hatchway at the side of our door and the food was slid on to the worktop; no one knocked to announce the arrival, the food just arrived. The TV announced that a hurricane had occurred at the village we had visited the previous evening, and a considerable amount of damage had been caused, some bungalows having lost their roofs.

We had suffered a very wet night; the yard outside flooded in no time; the noise on the tin roof kept us awake; neither of us had much sleep. I have never experienced such heavy rain; it continued most of the morning, so we spent time reading and sewing. The tour to see the whales was cancelled; the sea was still too rough after the hurricane, so the boats would not take the tourists out there.

At lunchtime we drove to Elliott Heads, still windy but warm; we only needed short sleeves for the rest of the day. Some of the time was spent on the beach round the rocks to see what could be found. There were many types of shells and coloured pebbles; we took time to examine then closely, particularly the unusual shapes. The river mouth was at one end of the beach, so we found some river creatures as well as sea. We took a different road back to the motel; the roads were very narrow, and the area was flat. Many places had been waterlogged the previous night with the heavy rain. The soil was very fertile; the main crop was sugar cane, but there was a large area with tomatoes.

For dinner that night we went to Bundaberg to the serviceman's club. The meal was 'half serve', which was a way of producing a meal at a cheaper rate for pensioners. We still had roast pork and helped ourselves to vegetables and salad; the portions were only slightly smaller than the ordinary size. The meal only cost us £2.50 each in English money. Rain had started to fall again by the time we returned to the motel.

What a night we had; I do not think I have ever seen so much lightning everywhere; it was lit up brilliantly, as it was mostly sheet lightning. We tried to watch the film *Indiana Jones* but there was too much noise with the weather. It also kept me from sleeping as the rain fell on the corrugated roof over the car; it was deafening. Three inches fell in no time.

October 1 already; they say time flies when you are enjoying yourself! but we had several hundred miles to travel. In the morning paper it stated that parts of Victoria had had heavy rain and storm damage overnight. On the way to Rockhampton Dennis got stopped by the police for speeding; needless to say he was not happy. The Gladstone police fined him $180, a set fine. Afraid I did not offer to pay! But he had the option to pay higher up the coast; it was all in the state of Queensland, as by now we had left New South Wales behind.

The town of Rockhampton was very pleasant and we enjoyed looking round. Our motel was on the main road to town, so it was easy to find. Most motels were alike including the names – this was 'Centre Point', with standard-type rooms – and all motels had a laundry, which we found very useful. The further north we travelled the warmer it appeared, hence the more we needed to change and wash our clothes.

Later in the day we drove up a winding road, with some hairpin bends and steep gradients, to the top of Mount Archer. It was worth reaching the top as we could see for miles. The top was covered in trees, wild plants and shrubs; a few birds were singing as they retired to bed. A young couple had joined us to watch the beautiful sunset. The colour was like a sunset in England when it was to be followed by a frosty night!

Another serviceman's club was found in the town for our evening meal. Dennis was able to have a game of snooker (which he won!). On returning to the motel plans were made for the following day.

It seemed all Australians, even when on holiday, got up early, possibly to avoid the heat of the day. We had breakfast at 8am and were the last to sit down for breakfast! Something else: Australians think nothing of travelling hundreds of miles in one day. Many roads are straight, with no bends, including in the centre of the country. I remember early on when we were touring with Beryl and Ray, Beryl wanted to see her sister who was *only* two hours down the road. If people wished to see someone they just travelled no matter the distance. It might even take a week to get there! Time in Australia is very much 'tomorrow, tomorrow', not now!

As we were in need of cash again, we left early. Banks first and then there was a large catalogue shop in the centre where goods were quite cheap. In fact Dennis bought two pairs of trousers for less than £10; these were good quality; after returning to England he wore them continually. He often said he wished he had bought more. Silk scarves were 50p each, tea towels 30p and teenagers' pants 20p! Nowhere had we seen anything cheaper; even in Singapore the clothes were more expensive. Later in the day I got my sewing needle out and shortened the new trousers, so that he could wear them while still on holiday.

It was from here we decided at short notice to alter the route north; instead we turned west towards Emerald. The temperature was rising quickly; we needed to wear hats as the sun was so strong. It was not known at the time but this was the beginning of the most interesting part of the tour. There were stretches of road that were so straight we could see for miles ahead, with undulations in the road, and so little traffic. We were more or less on our own.

Signs were along the road every little way directing us to Mount Hay. We did not know the significance so decided to find out. When we stopped there we were shown into a special show room that had masses of polished stones; they were called 'thunder eggs' and were taken from the ground in Mount Hay. Various sizes were on show, the average being two to three inches across, and egg-shaped, hence the name. If you paid $5 you could go and dig your own on the site. Once dug up you took them to a shed where the owners of the site would cut them open with special saws. Some had the most gorgeous colours and contained crystals, and could be polished. Visitors often took one half and left the second half for the owners to polish and sell. An easy way of making money while someone else had done the hard work! This was an interesting stopping point.

The railway ran parallel to the main road from Rockhampton. There were coal mines further west, some trucks towed by the trains carrying a considerable weight when full. According to the signs on the side of the trucks, we estimated that each truck had up to 30 tons. Several trains had one engine at the front and two in the centre of the train. The whole train had as many as 114 trucks. I had never seen one so long! I remember when in New South Wales we were told that one train could cope with as many as 200 trucks! In one place four-wheeled vehicles were being driven along the railway lines with front and rear rollers fitted; this was in connection with repairing the rails.

Progressing further west it was getting more outback, still a higher temperature, and cacti were growing along the side of the road, not just inches high but several feet high! More scrubland and the hills left behind. In patches, some Shorthorn, Hereford and Brahmin cattle were grazing where they could. Owing to the climatic conditions the Brahmin did well as they originated from India.

Eventually Emerald town came into view, where we stayed the night. There were people looking after the motel while the owners were away. The caretakers were English, but had been in Australia for 20 years. This was the way they toured the country learning and seeing more of Australia. As usual we found a serviceman's club for the evening meal. This time there was a difference as the standard was much lower, including plastic tablecloths, but we came for the food, not tablecloths! There were snooker and pool tables at the club so Dennis enjoyed more games. Quite interesting conversations arose about the locality. I had seen some emeralds and sapphires in the local shop windows earlier in the day. We were told if we continued to drive west we would come to two towns, Sapphire and Rubyvale, where it would be possible to go 'fossicking' (searching) for our own gems.

The following morning I took a walk to the local railway station as it had been preserved as it had been built in 1900. The local people were so proud of this building, there was no mistaking of when it had been built. No one was around so I walked along the platforms. Tropical plants were in hanging baskets and pots all along the platform. It was the best-kept building in town.

One reason for travelling in this direction was to visit a small town called Claremont to see a friend who had lived next door to us in the past. That evening we made a telephone call, only to be told she had moved to Mackay, but we decided to remain on the route planned.

Sapphire was approximately 25 miles from Emerald. It could not really be called a village, let alone a town, according to our standards! Most buildings were corrugated shacks. Only one shop, one petrol pump, and a caravan with one person selling gems. She was of a gypsy type, who would have told your fortune back in England. She was hoping for tourists The only brick-built shop, with air conditioning, belonged to the fire warden. He too was trying to sell some gems in a professional way.

We heard a mechanical digger at work so went to investigate. It was digging about 30 feet deep in the ground and filling a trailer with the soil. When this was full the operator disappeared, towing the trailer. He was one of the 'greedy' owners who used mechanics, so we were told. The trailers were taken to more machinery to wash and shake out the soil and rocks, hoping to find either rubies or sapphires. This was how he made his living.

At the end of the road was a caravan park; it was very rough; caravans were old and dilapidated, some having lean-to sheds attached. There was a very small shop, covering about two square yards! I think it only contained cold drinks; these were in proper sealed bottles; that was about all available to purchase! Apparently people came to their caravans at weekends just to go fossicking for gems, living in hopes they would make their fortune.

We then came to Rubyvale where we heard and then found the machine working; the man on duty welcomed us, and told us about his work. This was one of the places where the trailer came and tipped its spoil. The hopper was loaded and large rocks were pushed to one side; smaller ones were washed in a large purpose bath. There were then different stages of washing and grading, finally down to tiny stones. The gentleman put his hand in the last bath and pulled out a handful of gravel, and picked out some sapphire and ruby gemstones and also some small pieces of gold, which had been mixed in with the rubble. He gave Dennis two or three small gems.

There was a pile of unsorted boulders, stones and gravel where we could look for any gems and keep anything of value we found. It was so hot perspiration was running down our faces, although we were wearing hats. They were a must! We stayed for over an hour and found some very small gems. We later learnt that the temperature had been 38°C.

We then felt we would like a cold drink. We spied a galvanised shed not far away; it had a large sign advertising cold drinks. They were kept in a refrigerator, so we really enjoyed them. From the outside it looked more like a cattle shed, but the sign drew us there.

Later we visited the owner of all the machinery we had watched; they lived in a large bungalow, with another 'outside room' covered in netting so we were in the shade, also free of snakes. Here we were presented with more cold drinks and shown buckets full of gems; they had to be sorted by size ready for selling. We had never seen so many all at once; we just thought of the value! Some gems were for sale, so out came the owner's magnifying glass to study them; we actually purchased one each. This sounds very insignificant but they were expensive even to us.

By now it was 4pm and when darkness fell it was quick as there was no twilight. There were a further 87 kilometres to travel to Claremont. It was only in that town hotel rooms were available, none in Rubyvale or Sapphire.

We had hired a brand new car and the road on which we travelled was just track; this took us through the bush, no houses, no farms and no traffic. Some parts of the road were wet, with deep wheel ruts; in fact the extreme centre of the road was the best place to travel. The road was really for four-wheel drive vehicles, not a brand new car! It had also started to get dark before we left the track. I was literally sitting on the edge of my seat for the whole of the 87 kilometres! This was a *long* way. I was so relieved on reaching some tarmac road; Dennis just sat and laughed but I was a nervous wreck!

It was a lovely quiet hotel in Claremont. Dennis unfortunately did not feel well for two days so he spent time in bed; I walked around the town and just relaxed. We were told the temperature could rise as high as 50°C in the height of summer; thankfully we had arrived in spring. I found someone who knew the person we wanted to see, so stopped and had a long talk with her.

It did not seem possible it was already October 5. Dennis had almost used all his inhalers for asthma, so decided to see a doctor before travelling further. It cost him £14 for the prescription, then when arriving at the chemist he found he could have purchased them over the counter for much less money! Dennis was not particularly happy! When we paid the account at the hotel we were told it was to be a noisy weekend, as a young party was arriving, so we had obviously chosen the right time to stay.

We occasionally stopped and filmed the scenery en route to Mackay as this was different to what we had previously seen. There was very tall coarse grass and low bushes close to the road. The small trees were further from the road, along with some hills that reminded me of tall anthills, peaks at the top and about 200 feet high. Beef cattle were grazing any grass they could find. They probably had hundreds of acres to roam. Much of the road was so straight it was possible to see for miles ahead, just like the Bruce Highway. A few vehicles were travelling in either direction; this was one of the highways to the west. The nearer we were to Mackay the more fertile the ground, with crops of barley or bearded wheat; the crops were almost ready to harvest. At a guess the fields were approximately 100 acres each. I had seen this size just west of Sydney.

The temperature had risen to 32°C, and the journey from Claremont was 279 kilometres. It was pleasant to arrive along the coast to the warm breeze; this gave the impression that it was a few degrees cooler. The motel had been booked in advance before leaving Claremont; once again it was easy to find as it was on the main road. The motels were under separate ownership but mostly had the same layout including a laundry. With high temperatures laundries were very welcome so we were able to have more clean clothes. Most motels served breakfast but dinners had to be found elsewhere.

Bernice, the former neighbour from England, found us at the motel and took us to meet her brother and sister-in-law. They had a fish and chip shop, which was very popular. Yes, we had fish and chips for supper! A variety of fish was placed on our plates so that we could taste the fish of the area. Squid was one, which I found like chewing rubber, and with no particular taste, certainly a seafood I would not want again! Sweetlip and fillet of prawn were beautiful. The prawns were so large owing to the warm water where they lived. Many others were tasty, but names escape me. After catching up on all the news since Bernice had left England, it was midnight before we left for the motel.

Now Sunday October 6: a lazy morning after the late night. We were checking the films we had taken on the way; it was surprising how much film we had used. There would be plenty of editing when we returned home.

We met Bernice down at Mackay Harbour; we could see a few islands off the coast, and masses of sandy beaches, when we travelled to a bay outside the town. There were only one or two places one could actually go on to the beach owing to the steep cliffs. We watched the sun set over the sea, but before it finally set, there was an unusual colour on the sea near the beach. We were told this was caused by seeds released by the coral; these were floating for 15 or 20 feet from the shore. This happens about the same time every year.

The evening meal was in a restaurant and was remembered if only for the bad service. Dennis had to return his plate; we were not even offered a sweet or coffee, but then decided it was better to retire to bed.

Next morning Dennis was wide awake, it was breakfast and then back on to the Bruce Highway in a northerly direction for the next stop of Townsville. We had lunch at Bowen. At Townsville Dennis found two rooms for us in the Robert Towns Motel. This overlooked a very large church. The motel was on a hill, and when looking outside we could see the harbour which was very busy. I remembered visiting Magnet Island on a previous visit and being seasick! A few minutes' drive from the motel was Castle Hill, which was a terrific viewpoint. The road was narrow and winding as well as steep. The soil was a sandy orange colour. Some viewpoints were marked and had safety barriers as there were sheer drops to the bottom.

We were always ready for the evening meals after the day travelling a long distance, but as the cost of the evening meal at the motel was expensive we decided to drive around town and found a Sizzlers restaurant. This was self-service; you could eat as much as you wanted with no extra charges. The food was presented very well and a good selection. One thing that surprised us was the two tables close to us. We did not think they had eaten all the week, plates piled high and then back for second helpings for each course! They had their money's worth! We joked about the family afterwards.

The next day we made another visit to the bank as Dennis had to pay his fine at the town hall; needless to say I kept quiet. We parked the car at a meter and it cost us ten cents, somewhat cheaper than in England. Now it was back on to the Bruce highway; the road surface was poor, more like the C category roads in England, badly maintained, potholes, tree roots raising the tarmac, narrow road, just sufficient space for two lorries to pass. There was wild bushland either side of the road, with large termite mounds; they were from two to eight feet high.

Two pipelines ran parallel to the road for miles outside Townsville; they finally disappeared up a hill; we later learnt they contained water for the town. The area around was very dry and water had to be found for the town.

In Ingham we had a break to enjoy an ice cream; Australia has some delicious flavours, and my mouth waters as I write about it! This village had grown from a few houses to quite a large village, since I had last seen it a few years ago.

I insisted on visiting Mission Beach where I had been before, but so much had changed in the last eight years since I had stayed there. Even the large hotel had been extended and there were many new houses. We decided to stop and cool our feet in the sea; the water was warm and the beach sandy.

Innisfail was the next town on the way north; this had changed from a small hamlet to a town. The petrol tank was low so we stopped to fill up. The petrol was 73 cents per litre, the equivalent of 35 pence at home.

We reached Cairns after a journey of 404 kilometres. An Italian lady ran the hotel where we booked in. We visited the night market we had seen before along the promenade, but were told that it was the last night as it was closing for rebuilding, so only a few stalls were there. The pier had opened a large shopping mall, which remained open until late in the evening.

It rained all night and neither of us had much sleep as there was a tin outside the two bedrooms and all we heard was the 'drip, drip' all night. The following day it rained the whole time, so we decided we had had enough of Cairns and drove to Kuranda, still in the wet and very heavy rain; late evening on the television it stated there had been 11 inches of rain that day. It had not rained for 14 weeks before our arrival! We noticed the road to Atherton had been greatly improved, with less bends and potholes.

In the evening we revisited Atherton and the Hinterland Motel, only with different owners this time. It was pleasant bringing back memories from the first visit. The previous time we had come the pub was derelict, but this time it had been refurbished and become a thriving business, serving some very tasty meals. After rain and sleepless nights we had an early night.

Next morning we were up with the birds; they were really in song and ready for the new day. It was decided we would drive over the planes to Yungaburra. We stopped to look at the gems in the shop which we found in 1992. The owner was very interesting to talk to as he mined his own gems in north Queensland. He brought back large rocks, and broke them down to see any gems inside. Opals in particular were cut and polished and set in jewellery. He also had opal stones ready to mount. I selected one from a box he brought out, telling me how much they would cost. I chose a stone; he then said it should have been in a more expensive box, but still let me have it for the price originally quoted. I have wondered since if he was just trying to make out that I had a more expensive stone! My stone, a 'black opal', was set in a gold ring, but the ring had to be enlarged. We returned the next day to collect it.

Close by was the enormous fig tree. The roots were large and draped down the host tree; it had grown up inside the trunk. Coaches stopped here to view the largest tree in the area, very difficult to describe. There were sketches and information for tourists to study.

After travelling on some back roads we came to Malanda; Dennis found an art gallery, and after a picture had been taken out of the frame he brought it home. On his return to England it was reframed and hung in his bedroom until he died.

Millaa Millaa had to be visited again, particularly the garage where we had made friends with Patsy and her family last time. Patsy and Leslie owned the garage. Leslie was still breeding some of the wild birds; some of them were very rare. Patsy suggested Leslie take us down to Millaa Millaa Falls to view and listen to wildlife. Leslie was an expert although only 18. In the stream we saw a duck-billed platypus, and also a large water dragon; unfortunately it moved too quickly to photograph. Leslie was so keen that we should see as much as possible. Even at this stage he had been taking part in research and hoped to continue these studies, and possibly be a game warden. This was such an interesting day, and weather sunny and warm.

Back at Atherton for the evening we found a large quilting exhibition in a room at the back of the pub. Neither of us had seen such beautiful work, so we spent some time admiring it. The local people had got together as a club and showed so many articles. Not only cushion covers, but tablecloths, wall murals, table centres, bedspreads and toys. When we left I found a bright green frog on the windowsill outside croaking. We knew bright-coloured frogs could be poisonous so let it well alone.

The room where Dennis was staying at the Hinterland had masses of ants when we returned. We sprayed with a repellent, and Dennis did not go to bed until he thought they had all been treated.

We drove to Barrina Lake, which was supposed to be bottomless; it had been formed from an old volcano. Here wild turkeys were running round in the car parks clearing up food left by visitors. Pleasure boats were taking trips round the lake; wildlife was prolific, both on the water and on land. Although visitors were around it was a very peaceful area. There was the usual gift shop, with expensive items.

As time was passing it was time to make our way towards Cairns. On the way there were some beautiful views as we passed over the mountains, but we did stop for lunch, at a pub where we had stopped in 1992. After lunch we walked down to the river; there were fish and turtles, they enjoyed being fed and came to the surface close to us. One more night was spent in Cairns in a hotel nearly opposite the one we had stayed at earlier.

The next day the car was checked and returned; the distance travelled had been 2185 miles since leaving Brisbane. This was worth all the money paid for the hire of the car, a real trip of a lifetime, to look back on with great memories. We had some film developed while waiting for our flight. New Zealand was the next place to visit.

Part 4: New Zealand

It was the beginning of another day and long journey. Again I had not slept much the previous night as I had to wake Dennis, in the next room. He did not like early mornings, and I was afraid of being late. The taxi took us to the airport for $6.90 at 4.15am. Our flight left at 6.50 for Auckland, just five hours in the air, and clocks were three hours ahead of Cairns, so a breakfast was provided on the way. The flight path took us down the coast to Brisbane and Sydney, crossing the sea to New Zealand.

Our friends John and Sheila came to meet us and waited until we collected our hire car. We followed them to their home; they had moved since the last visit. Daughter Kathy had been allowed to have a home built in their back garden. It was like our English mobile homes. The temperature was lower than Cairns so we soon felt the difference, in fact I shivered. John gave me a pullover and invited me to take back it home.

It was spring in NZ, and also election day, so this was under discussion in the evening. One thing I could not understand was Kathy calling her mother and father by their Christian names. The remainder of the day was spent catching up with the four years since we last saw them. After a good night's sleep we awoke to a wet and windy day; there was no encouragement to leave the house. When Kathy arrived we gave her the silver cutlery which she had asked us to take out for her.

The following day, we were on the move again to the Bay of Islands in the north. John led us on to the main highway, as he had shown us the route to travel. The weather was better and the trip was enjoyed, stopping at the famous sheep farm for coffee. We had purchased lunch on the way up. It was early evening

119

when we reached Paihia, and 150 miles later. As I had stayed here before I looked for the motel near Haruru Falls, but no luck. On the way we spotted another motel called 'Cook's Lookout', so we booked in there. This was in a beautiful position overlooking the large bay; we could also see Waitangi and the bridge. We had a holiday home which had an outside patio, where we spent much of our time. Dennis went sea fishing with the owner. Every convenience was there. We cooked meals. The car was parked just outside the home.

One day we brought lunch back from the town. It was a roast and plates were piled high; as there were two, the second plateful was enjoyed the next day. The weather was sunny and warm, so we spent much of the time just relaxing on the patio enjoying the views. Dennis unfortunately spent some of the time in bed as once again he was not feeling well. We watched the tide come in and out, leaving quite a large area of mud flats. Our binoculars were useful for spying anything which was out of the normal. People were digging for bait in the mud, fishing in small boats when the tide came in. Birds of many different species were flying around the area. At one stage there were canoeists, probably belonging to a local club; later when we went down to the bridge the canoes were all together.

We went down to Waitangi to study the view up to the motel; it was clearly visible on the top of the hill. Next we drove to a small bay, and during the afternoon we spent many hours on the beach, turning over small rocks and watching little spider crabs; there were thousands of them rushing around to get out of our sight. Some were no bigger than our thumbnail! There were three different types of starfish, many sea slugs, sea cucumbers (animal, not vegetable), prawns and hermit crabs.

While we were on the beach a Maori came down with a sack, picking something up from the water's edge; when she had finished, being nosey we wanted to know what she had been gathering. She called them sea potatoes; they looked like curled-up hedgehogs, covered in large thorns. They would have fitted in our hands. Maoris eat them raw; raw fish, no thank you!

After having seen enough of the shore, we drove back but stopped to photograph plants and shrubs in bloom. The tea trees were in flower, and eventually we arrived at Haruru Falls. The next day Dennis was not really interested in travelling the western side of North Island, but I persuaded him, knowing what the scenery was like. The trip took us through Pakaraka, Ohaeawai, Kaikohe and to Opononi. The scenery became more beautiful the further west we travelled. Hills, valleys with beef cattle grazing and many orchards containing apples, oranges, avocados and vines. Opononi was just a small village on a bay, with large sand dunes. The day we visited there were heavy large rolling waves.

Typical New Zealand view

Lunch was in a small friendly café close to the beach. Beef stew and lasagne was very tasty. Afterwards we saw a fish and chip shop, but the smell was sufficient to put anyone off buying from there; besides it looked dirty. It was the first time I had seen a cylindrical building housing public toilets. It was metal and even the door was curved. I have travelled many miles but had never seen one before.

Plants grew down to the sea, two or three different varieties were in bloom and had succulent leaves, but not a seaweed. The sea was trying to gain here, so hundreds of old tyres were supporting the sand bank. While we were there a group of councillors were discussing the problems and how to improve the situation, but money budgeted for other things was to be used for sea defences.

Unfortunately Dennis had dropped his new camera and the strap had broken; as it was under guarantee he would get it repaired back in Singapore. We did continue on to the beautiful woods where the largest kauri tree in New Zealand stood; it is called 'Tane Mahuta'. The size is very impressive; it takes 16 people holding hands to go round the trunk. Other trees contained many ferns growing on branches and trunks. The complete day trip was 70 miles. We arrived back in time for Dennis to book a fishing trip at sea, for the next day.

Woodland with ferns

While Dennis was sailing I walked around the town of Paihia, as I do not have 'sea legs'. I also walked along the beach but could not stay long as sand midges kept biting my legs. Dennis arrived back as it was getting dark having had an interesting day. One of the fishermen on his trip was the owner of the motel where we were staying. Dennis had caught three large fish, giving one to the motel owner; we were told they were snappers. I cooked one for our evening meal, then saved the large fish to take back to our Auckland friends. Other men on board the fishing boat caught barracuda which apparently was not fit to eat; they are normally full of worms. The fishermen had to return some of the fish to the sea as they were the wrong size to take to the shore. There are strong regulations regarding the size. The fresh air really did Dennis a lot of good.

Next morning everything had to be packed and cleared by 10am. We went to the office and paid, and were invited for a cup of coffee before leaving. A long conversation took place about the previous day's fishing and also 'the one that got away' on other trips.

It was now time to make the tour back to Auckland; as usual Dennis drove, breaking speed limits as normal. We stopped in Wellsford for coffee and to fill the car with petrol. One thing we noticed was that the cost per litre was rising the further south we went. In Paihia it was 77 cents per litre and by the time we reached Auckland it was 90 cents; apparently the main oil refinery was in the north of the island.

While in Wellsford we looked in estate agents, looking at prices; there were several reasonable but one took our fancy, $80,000 (£40,000), a three double-bedroom bungalow with a large plot of ground, approximately three acres, double garage and other outbuildings. Farms over here would cost three or four times this amount of money. We ended back in Pakuranga (a suburb of Auckland), and John and Sheila were out, so we spent the time sitting on their balcony, in a temperature of 22°C.

There was a great welcome when our friends arrived back home. After the evening meal we showed them some film we had taken and they both fell asleep! Very interesting film!

The following day John took Dennis out for a ride in the car, while Sheila and I stopped at home to gossip. Sunday we were given instructions to be up early, so that we could visit the flea market at Mount Wellington. This was the same as a car boot sale in England, only so much smaller. I bought a small china plate with an Australian pea flower painted on it. The next stop our 'taxi' made was to Cornwall Park where John had worked in his earlier days. Sheep and cattle grazed in the park between clumps of various species of trees. Sir Logan Campbell originally owned the park, and in early days it was used purely for farming; when he died, it was kindly donated to the people of Auckland. It contained the famous One Tree Hill. Incidentally the one tree was supported by braces as Maoris tried to cut it down in a protest in 1994. This of course caused the tree to be completely cut down later as it died.

The park still had large holes where volcanic eruptions occurred years ago, but now they were covered with grass. Boulders thrown by the volcanic activity were quite large and lay around on the ground after all these years.

The two houses where Sir Logan had lived were open to the public as museums. One, called Acacia Cottage, was built in the mid-nineteenth century and still contained some original furniture. The newer house had more rooms, but they were no bigger than in the cottage; this one was two storeys high and contained five bedrooms. Each room was lined with wood, including ceilings and floors. As usual any tourist place had a café and refreshments, including ice creams. The ice creams here had real strawberries plus real cream, very fattening but delicious. John afterwards took us back by travelling a different way to the town.

Sheila made some delicious date scones for tea; the recipe included melting the margarine, plenty of milk plus an egg, beat this thoroughly before adding the self-raising flour, then cook in a hot oven: great! John had Sky TV so we watched some American programmes before retiring for the night.

Early next morning was the weekly shopping expedition, so the week's groceries were purchased. It was interesting comparing prices with those in England. Shoes were very expensive, anything from £50 to £100, nothing cheaper. The men disappeared together while Sheila and I went into the supermarket. Biscuits were much more expensive than in England, there was little difference in the price of meat, milk was 60 pence per litre, paper products were also considerably more costly. A very interesting morning costing items of the two countries. On the way back to Pakuranga, the discussion continued. Community tax appeared higher, and purchasing a house in Auckland meant a high price. This was our last day in New Zealand.

We had to fill the petrol tank on the way back to returning the car at the airport. We lost John who was supposed to be showing us the way to the airport, so we just followed the signs. We had travelled 971 kilometres. When we arrived we paid the airport tax, said goodbye to our friends. This time was the last time we saw them as they have since passed on.

Booking in at the airport was not easy, as it was declared our names were not on the flight. We had telephoned the previous day and been told all was well. We eventually took off to Singapore after waiting for three hours. Food on the New Zealand airways was superb, as we had found on an earlier tour. Not long after this a stewardess took us to the cockpit to meet the captain and his co-pilot and to look at the controls. Dennis had a flying license, so was so interested in everything. I had also always wanted to have a look in the cockpit, but did not have the courage to ask.

I add a postscript to this only to say entering the cockpit is no longer allowed owing to the troublemakers.

Tane Mahuta, the largest living kauri tree in New Zealand (height 51.5m, girth 13.8m).

Part 5: Singapore Again

When we arrived at the airport in Singapore it was 9.30pm and dark; from here we took another taxi out to the Garden hotel where we had stayed on the way out to Australia. On the way we passed an area with fairy lights all in the trees. This was Little India and it was a special religious time as they were celebrating the 'Festival of Light'; the official date was November 10, but celebrations go on for several weeks. The festival means good over evil, light over darkness. Hindu temples and homes have coloured lights. The whole area comes alive at this time of year, with pulsating rhythms, and everyone wears their best clothes. We decided to make a visit to this area of Singapore the following evening.

Once again breakfast was in the hotel where we had stayed on the way out, where there was a choice of continental style or cooked. After this we had to find the plaza to mend Dennis's camera strap. Repairs had to be carried out here owing to the guarantee. I also purchased a pair of leather shoes for £14. They were not easy to find as the local people had such small feet. Many watches and rings had well-known stamped names but it was doubtful they were genuine as stamped. A Rolex for £20?

We walked until we were worn out! So we hailed a taxi to return to the hotel. The remainder of the afternoon we sat on a balcony bird watching. We saw a kingfisher and also an oriole.

After a sleepless night I was up early; my internal clock had not caught up with Singapore time, as there were five hours' difference between Singapore and New Zealand. When we arrived back in England, there would be a seven-hour difference between there and here.

This was the last day in Singapore, so we went to Little India, where we had previously passed through on our way to the hotel. Another taxi took us there, but there were difficulties as taxis have their own specific areas where they can travel in Singapore. There was a selection of materials with the most beautiful colours and embroidery. Enough material for a sari cost as little as £7. Many people were celebrating until late in the night, but we did not stop as we had a long journey the next day.

The television quoted the temperatures for London as 17°C and Auckland 28°C, Hong Kong 26°C. To us it had appeared much hotter when we first flew from England. It seemed strange as announcers on American TV were saying 'Good night', when it was already 8am with us in Singapore.

Most of the packing had been done the night before. There was a very heavy storm with thunder and lightning while we had breakfast, then the rain came like stair rods.

The taxi driver taking us to Changi airport gave us a commentary on the way. The last of our money was spent in the duty free shop before boarding the aircraft. The flights were delayed owing to the thunderstorms. It was 13 hours' flight to Heathrow. On our way home we travelled over the Arabian Gulf, and we saw some mountains in the distance. We arrived early morning when the taxi was waiting to take us to Ringwood and home.

So this was the last of our adventure; was it worth the trip? There is no doubt that the films will be played and replayed over the years to come. Dennis remarked he had one of the happiest days of his life while handling the birds in Burrinjuck National Park. As for me, there was not one day or incident that stands out as being the best, but the complete trip, and would I do it again? Oh yes, and a bit more!

A postscript: after returning to England we tried to emigrate to New Zealand, but as we were retired, and after paying for a home out there, we had insufficient money to live there. Also we unfortunately found Dennis had cancer of the liver; he died in 2000.

Boston, Massachusetts
May 1997
(one week)

I breed King Charles Cavalier dogs; I had some puppies at the time, and an American lady living in Vermont heard about them and asked her brother to visit, knowing they were for sale. After a considerable amount of correspondence she bought a pup, and the result was a trip to America to take the pup over safely by air. There were massive regulations to go through, vets' injections etc. before we finally left England.

He arrived safely, travelling very well in the special hold in the aircraft. I filled his water bowl with ice cubes so he had continual fresh water to drink. While we were collecting our luggage he arrived on the next conveyer belt. The new owners met us at the airport, paying for the pup at the same time; I had also taken some clean bedding, so although in a strange place he had something he knew. We handed Drummer over to the new owners. He was now four months old; I would not allow him to travel while younger. On the proceeds of this I had a holiday with a friend in and around Boston.

Rosemary and I took a taxi to our hotel which was on the outskirts of the city. The driver realised we were tourists here for the first time, so acted as a guide, pointing out places of interest on the way to the 'Midtown hotel'. We tried to find a tourist agent as Rosemary wanted to visit Niagara Falls but found it was too far to travel.

One thing I found quite amazing: I forgot to bring headache pills and so went to a chemist. I had never seen so many different makes; I had to ask the pharmacist to guide me!

Mum with babies

DRUMMER
EXPORTED TO
AMERICA

Drummer

Owing to the change of time from England to America we went to bed extra early. As the result of the early night we were awake early – to rain! Directly opposite us was the headquarters of the Christian Scientist Church, and the carillion was playing hymn tunes as it was Sunday morning, quite a novelty.

After breakfast we purchased a ticket for the 'Orange bus'; this had 19 stops on the circuit. A bus arrived every half hour, and was an 'on-off', so this enabled us to see much of the city. The ticket only cost $14. The first stop was at a wharf where the Boston Tea Party was celebrated. We listened to the information about how it originated. A boat carried tea and to avoid taxes the tea was dumped over the side in the water! All this occurred in the late eighteenth century; a museum at the site showed all details of how it happened.

We returned to the bus for the famous Quincy Market, and this was all under cover. There was a large walking space down the centre with stalls on either side. In the food hall there was a considerable selection of food including carvery meals, pizzas, ice cream, cakes, bread, bagels, fruit, fish, sausages and fruit drinks, each stall having its own speciality. There was little space to sit and eat except under a large dome in the centre. Here were heavy wooden tables and benches for the public to sit and eat. It was noticed everyone cleared their own rubbish. Outside the food hall stalls were placed with objects of all descriptions to sell souvenirs.

After this we completed the bus circuit back to the hotel. The driver kept making typical American jokes which he thought were funny – but not to us! In the evening we watched TV in the hotel as there were special memorial programmes; these particularly dwelt on families left behind after husbands, fathers and brothers had been killed during wars.

The following day it was time to explore the 'subway', the underground train system. It only cost us 85 cents for the day, and we could travel anywhere. There were five different coloured lines but they were easy to follow. Our stop was at the park, where we walked and visited some large shopping stores, two of which had clothes for sale. Some articles had as much as 70% marked down from the original price. These prices did not include tax so we had that to pay on top of the quoted price.

We completed our shopping and walked back to the park where entertainment was provided. A large church choir were singing, unaccompanied, many pieces we knew. Rosemary purchased an ice cream for 50 cents plus tax. It was enormous, almost a meal! We took the subway back to the street outside the hotel, where we found a food market so bought some chicken for dinner.

The following day we used the subway again, only this time to a wharf, close to the boats which took us on a 'whale watch'. It cost $32 each to go on the trip. We were warned that the sea may be choppy; this did not worry me as I had taken tablets to stop seasickness before leaving the hotel. After leaving the harbour it was said we may have to turn back as the sea was going to get rougher. The chairs were sliding about the deck; it was a case of holding on. The chairs were plastic, like some of our garden chairs. A leg on my chair snapped off; the same fate befell a passenger behind me. Rosemary tried to stop me falling and cut her hand in the process, in fact she carries the scar today. This type of chair would not be allowed in England.

The whale area was reached and the boat turned, only for me to receive the smell of the fumes; unfortunately this finished me. I did carry some plastic bags, and did I need them? I finished on my knees with one hand stuck in the air with the camera trying to obtain some photos, and the plastic bag in the other. I found later that I did manage to take some photographs. I will not be going out again! I understand very few passengers remained on their feet. This was quite an experience, and I did manage to see the whales. I really felt weak for the rest of the day! So back to the hotel.

A location where Boston Pops concerts were held was just round the corner from the hotel; unfortunately we chose the wrong dates to be there! A visit was made to the Christian Scientist Church, an enormous place with extremely high ceilings, which could seat 2000 people. The organ had four manuals and 1500 pipes. It must have been beautiful to hear the church filled with a massive sound of music. The church and all buildings surrounding it belonged to the Christian Scientists movement. Inside was a large grandfather clock made in Britain by a family called Budgen. Upstairs we had a map of the world on the walls around us. Quite fascinating to find we were standing inside the world.

The next day we went on the subway to the coach station as we intended to visit Plymouth; this was a 40 minute drive along the motorway in a southerly direction. We passed many acres of woodland, with trees in their spring colours, also some wooden houses scattered along the route.

The coach left us in a coach park and we took a taxi to the plantation. This was where the Mayflower first landed from England, and was now set up as a working village museum; people were working in costume and using tools of the 1600s. As you walked round you would come across someone working with either old tools or even their hands, wearing the costume of that period. They even talked in an old English dialect. School children were asking questions as they met up with the workers. Houses were built in a similar style to the time the Mayflower immigrants arrived in what was to be the town of Plymouth. It was possible to see cobblers, carpenters, gardeners and potters all at work. We spent several hours walking around, and then travelled in another taxi to see the Plymouth Rock and a replica of the Mayflower.

Ocean Spray was where cranberries had been made popular although actual farms were away from the main buildings. Films showed how and where they grew in wet fields, and after being picked were made into drinks and jams, sometimes mixed with other fruits. They had a very large business with England. My favourite was cranberry and raspberry; since returning home I have drunk gallons! After this we returned to Boston; the weather had been beautiful with a temperature of 21°C.

Once again an early start as we had decided to take the 'Duck' tour around the town. A 'Duck' was the term used for amphibious vehicles; this took us on a tour around the town first, and then on to the river. This gave us the opportunity to see Boston from a different angle. Rosemary was invited to take over the steering of the vehicle while we were on the river. Our driver pointed out how many of the roads were in the process of being put underground, with the cost of billions of dollars.

As this was our last full day in America this time, we made it a restful day! This is always the way we like to end our many tours.

The evening meal we ate in the hub restaurant; this was 52 floors up, quite expensive with real cordon bleu food, very nice and a pleasant extra treat.

The last morning it was 'up early' as our taxi was coming for 6.15am, and it was only 20 minutes to the airport. In Boston rush hour commences at 6.30am, so we needed to start early to miss most of this. This part of the country is so different to Florida or Los Angeles; an interesting time and well spent!

Plymouth museum

Bergen, Norway
July 2000
(day trip)

This was just a day tour taken from Bournemouth airport on my own. Palmair had been running these tours, and Bergen was a place I had not visited. Those taking the tour started booking in at 6am and returned later in the day. The flight took two hours including a good breakfast en route; this helped as a large lunch was not required, especially as an evening meal was supplied on the way home!

Coaches met us at the airport with a guide. The guide spoke perfect English; she had been to England to perfect her English language. During the tour she consistently told us how much each house would cost, when up for sale. The scenery was gorgeous with mountains and the islands close to Bergen.

We were told about the history of Norway and how so much of the country was covered in mountains, making it difficult to visit other parts. Skiing was a tourist attraction, particularly for Danish people as their country is so flat. Norway was ruled by Danmark for many years, hence the old Norwegian language is similar to the Danish. The country has had monarchy for many centuries; the prince, next in line to the throne, was studying in Bergen at the time of our visit. He had a flat in one of the palaces on the outskirts of the city. There were beautiful gardens in the palace grounds; they were open for the public to view.

We visited a church which was built completely of wood; arsonists had burnt the church down in the early nineties, but a wealthy woman had it completely rebuilt exactly as it was in the past. She paid for the building eight years prior to our visit. The church was only small, and unusual compared to some churches. It was situated in a wood amongst trees away from the town. Christianity had been in Norway for the last thousand years; before that the people worshipped Nordic gods for about 4000 years. There was a cross on a mound outside the church; this was where the people had worshipped their gods in the past.

The coach took us to many viewpoints. Some houses had been built in the lower ground during the last 50 years; our guide remembered cattle grazing on this ground before the building took place. Many of the older houses were built on the high ground, typically Scandinavian; by that I mean with Danish and Swedish influence. There were narrow cobbled streets in the older part of town. Edvard Grieg had lived in a house in the old town where he composed much of his music.

Germany took over the country during the 1939–45 war. Standing on one side of the fjord, we were shown where a boat had been anchored on the opposite side, near the houses, in 1944; the Germans filled the boat with explosives and it was detonated, causing a considerable amount of damage. The anchor was blown on to the top of the mountain, and many people were killed. Close to this area was a large cemetery where kings of Norway were buried.

Near the centre of the city was a large market, and many of the stalls contained fish of all descriptions, fresh, dried, smoked, filleted, heads for soup. Some were made into snacks of fish with bread rolls to eat in the street. There were a few fruit and vegetable stalls. Other commodities included beautifully hand-knitted pullovers and jackets. The design and colours were breathtaking, but they were extremely expensive, too much for my pocket!

Several of us took the funicular railway to the top of the mountain. A marvellous view was had from there. The hotel provided meals for non-residents as well as residents. Just think of the view, if staying there! Many islands could be seen from here and several were occupied. A boat went round to the inhabited islands and provided a mobile cinema, as this was the only chance of seeing films here.

Back down in the small cobbled streets I visited the cathedral; it was old but gave the impression of a fairly new construction.

The atmosphere was very calming; it had many paintings of priests from the past. From here I walked to the centre of the city, to the war memorial; it was large, standing in the square, depicting the many who died during the last world war. The figures stood taller than a normal person.

Later in the day the coaches collected us, just as it started to rain, and we returned to the airport and home. This was my first trip to Norway, and yes I would like to return!

Riga, Latvia
July 2000
(day trip)

Another day out without complaints! The usual booking in and waiting for take-off. Yes, another breakfast on the way, on the two-hour flight to Riga. We circled the town before landing. We passed through a little of the countryside in a coach before going into the town. Farms were small with strips of crops not unlike those in Danmark a few years ago. Houses were in poor condition and needing a coat of paint.

As we got nearer to the town we stopped at a suspension bridge built in 1985, of which the Latvians were justly proud. In some ways it was not unlike the original bridge over the English River Severn just north of Bristol. From this point we looked down the river and could see some church spires on the other bank. The country had been overrun by communists until 1988; this had left the people very poor.

In the city Japan had donated an unusual clock; it had three faces on a pyramid, with one side having two faces, one giving the Japanese time. We spent nearly two hours walking through the streets looking at some of the original architecture, which had now been repaired. Some of the old buildings were beautiful, but I was glad to visit at this time as many of the communist buildings were being pulled down; they were poorly built. New ones were being installed to encourage tourists in the future.

We were told when the communists occupied Latvia they turned many houses into flats, cramming in many people, often one family in one room. The Russians needed houses for their staff and to run businesses and policing, over the 60 years they occupied the country. Some buildings built by the Russians were uninteresting, concrete square buildings. The churches were closed down as the Russians communists were against religion, but they did leave the fifteenth-century buildings. The main cathedral had part of the roof altered to place a hoist on which to lift sacks of corn; the place was used for storing the corn. Some churches were used as gymnasiums, in fact they were used for anything except religion. Some churches lost the paintings that were on the walls inside. The Russians painted over them with whitewash; most pictures were completely destroyed. Now restoration of the churches was taking place, the cathedral had an art exhibition, with country scenes.

In the square there were many small stalls selling gifts, including amber in all types of jewellery. Also some pictures with amber to embellish the scenes.

A very pleasant day out, but the people had suffered so much under communism, I felt they had a long way to go to get back to normal. Not a city I wish to return to!

Reykjavik, Iceland
August 2000
(day trip)

This time I had the company of Jenny, who had been one of my staff at work. We had an early start for the day trip. The flight took us over the western part of England and Wales at 29,000 feet, and then over part of Scotland. In all it took three hours to the main airport at Reykjavik. There were three coaches waiting for our flight, and each with a guide who spoke good English. They took us sightseeing for the day

A little of the history of the country was explained so that it was possible to understand some of the development, and how they were situated just south of the Arctic Circle. There are over 100 volcanoes in Iceland, with fields of lava which cover hundreds of square miles, and numerous hot springs. The climate is fairly mild considering the position. Apparently the temperature is warmer now than when our guide was a child. The temperature for us was 21°C. The people had their origin mostly from the Scandinavian countries, particularly Norway, but some from Greenland, which is the nearest land on the north-western side of Iceland, and approximately 250 kilometres away. The country only became independent from Danmark in 1944.

There was little crime in the country; I wondered if the reason is that the people are more 'God-fearing'. There were many Lutheran churches and some Catholic churches. Iceland has no army of its own, although during the 1939–45 war, after Germany invaded Danmark, the English army, navy and air force were stationed in the country. There were still some visible remains of the camps.

The houses had very Scandinavian architecture, with roofs having large overlaps at the eaves, and mostly made of wood. All the wood had to be imported and until recently there were no trees on the island. Now some spruce trees have been cultivated to withstand the climate. On the route from the airport to town, we passed very volcanic ground. The base of all the roads was volcanic ash. The main road was very straight as the ground was very flat; the mountains could be seen in the background on the eastern side. We later learnt the population lived only on the coastline, owing to the volcanic interior, where some volcanos were still active. Many earthquakes take place every year.

On the way we stopped to look at a Lutheran church, which was adjoining the President's house. It seemed amazing that there were no fences or guards outside his house, although we were asked to respect him and not go too close. In the cemetery all the graves were above ground owing to the lava rock.

As one would expect, money comes mainly from fishing for cod and herring and also much is exported; along the wharfs were a large number of fishing vessels. Everywhere was so clean, even the air smelt clean; you felt you wanted to take deep breaths! There was so little industry to pollute the air.

Other than fish most of the requirements for living were imported, hence everything was very expensive. There were no cattle and very few sheep, and they had to be kept under cover for the winter. In parts of the lowland the people were making hay, for the sheep and the many horses. The horses were of a very hardy breed, and several had been exported. Very few houses had a garden owing to the nonexistence of soil. An aluminium factory was on the outskirts of the town. This provided work for many people, and some of the product was exported. They used geothermal power to run the industry. There were no railways but many inland flights.

We were taken on a tour of the town showing us various beautiful churches and old houses. Many from our tour had lunch at a hotel but Jenny and I went to a supermarket and just bought a snack! This also gave us a chance to see what type of food the locals ate. There were very few shops in the town; it was more like an old-fashioned village! It did not seem possible it was the capital of Iceland.

Hallgrims Church was the largest church and had unusual architecture, with a bell tower and spire which was very high. At twelve o'clock the clock struck the hour, and the bells played a hymn tune for two or three minutes. Inside was very plain, modern and extremely light for a large church. It seemed strange with enormous clear windows behind the altar.

A house on the quay known as the municipal reception house was where the NATO treaty was agreed with the presidents of America and Iceland; they shook hands on the steps. This is now a popular place for tourists to visit and have photographs taken.

From here the coach took us up into the mountains for the afternoon. The roads were very narrow and made of volcanic ash; long stretches were under repair. The coach stopped at a lake, quite high in the mountains. It was uncanny as there was no wildlife and a complete silence. Not a bird in sight, no plants except for one or two small places where lichen was living. I have never been anywhere before that felt so completely dead; it was a most peculiar atmosphere.

Further along we stopped where a boiling mud pool was active; it just turned over, 'plop, plop', looking like a pond of porridge. As we looked up the side of the mountain – or I should say volcano! – it was possible to see the yellow sulphur with steam rising from the centre. There were several such places, some large with plumes of steam, and others just smouldering. It was in this area our Queen stood on a bridge over a pool, having a look round, and a month later the bridge was blown up by an earthquake. This area so reminded me of parts of New Zealand.

There was more lichen nearer the coast where we travelled. This variety grew up to about six inches high along the mountainside. The ground was very rugged where large rocks had been thrown out of the volcano; these were scattered covering a large area. We looked down to the lowland and saw some patches of farmland on the edge of the cliffs, where there was a sheer drop into the sea.

Before going home we visited the 'Blue Lagoon', where the water had an enormous amount of mineral content. The water came from the ground too hot for swimming so had to be cooled first, then heated to the correct temperature. All the houses on the island were heated from the natural resources in the winter months; this must have been a financial help.

The lagoon was very relaxing, and made the skin and legs really refreshed. I could feel the difference when flying home, although I only paddled there. Apparently people with illnesses come there for the natural treatment.

At least I can say I had a lovely day out, coming back with a little more knowledge of the country.

Marrakech, Morocco
May 2001
(day trip)

I flew again from Bournemouth, this time to Marrakech in Morocco, and without a companion! The car parks had changed and were easier to return to later in the day. Although I was wearing my old shoes they proved to be best for all the walking we did during the day. Before leaving the airport we all had to walk over mats with strong disinfectant as there was foot and mouth in England. We flew south over France, Spain and Gibraltar. It was possible to have a very clear view of the rock, although we were flying at 33,000 feet. By the time we had got this far breakfast had been eaten and cleared.

Over Moroccan parts of the desert, with little else but sand, the Atlas mountains on the eastern side. The nearer to Marrakech we came the more orange and olive groves were spotted; several orchards were in various states of growth, in other words with mature and young trees. They had been planted in neat rows. We could see holes in the ground, mostly in lines; later we learnt they were water wells for irrigation. They followed a dry river bed. We were informed that no rain had fallen for 11 months. The guide laughed when we told them we had had almost 11 months of continual rain, as it had been a very wet year.

The airport was very small, and we completed a visa on the way there, for immigration; also we were not allowed to take any food into the country owing to our foot and mouth. Two coaches awaited our arrival, each with a guide. The temperature was 21°C, but the previous week it had been nearly 38°C. The guides spoke fluent English; their normal second language was French, as

France had a large influence on the country. Signs everywhere were written in French and Arabic. Many French people had emigrated to Morocco.

We had to make the first stop at a bank as English currency was not accepted here. The dirham was the currency, and could not be obtained in England at that time. We were given a background to Moroccan history; kings were quoted back to 1000 AD. The main wall of the city dated back to this period. The first thing noticed was that everything had a very simple exterior, all painted in a hard pink colour. It was not possible to tell the difference between a house, mosque or palace from the outside. Many cars appeared old and rather dilapidated; masses of cycles were ridden through the streets, as were autocycles. Unsurprisingly many accidents occurred with cycles as the law of the road was not adhered to; we saw one happen when a cyclist was knocked off his cycle. He just got up and rode off to some shouting from the driver of the car, probably not repeatable words!

Abdel the guide took us sightseeing in the town, including a visit to the 'Jardin Majorelle'. It was named after Louis Majorelle, a son of a furniture maker, born in Nancy, France. He went to Marrakech in 1919 as a painter, acquired this land, landscaped it and called it the Majorelle Garden. It was opened to the public in 1947.

It is a mysterious garden, having so many shapes and forms with the plants, mostly cacti. There are some ordinary trees, but many cacti have grown as tall as them, with flowers on the branches. There were some like pin cushions, amongst the smaller varieties. One species grew about three foot high, like sticks with red flowers on the ends! Birds were flying freely and singing their spring song; they could be heard everywhere as the place was so quiet despite being in the city. The house was painted outside a royal blue, with fancy wrought iron guards for the windows and doors in bright yellow. The house is a museum and Yves St Laurent has established a trust to continue the existence of the house, garden and museum. Besides the cacti, bougainvilleas in pink and purple; these were prolific along an outer fence. The Moroccans are extremely proud of this garden as the area is so dry.

From here we visited the Bahia Palace; on arrival we found it was the old palace and not where the king resides, although parts were still used for government members to meet the king and also concubines. The guide seemed to revel in the concubines. We did learn they were taken at the age of 14 or 15 and kept there, unless they had a child. When a child was born the mother would move away to raise it but mothers had to leave, to return to normal life in the palace, when the children were old enough. In the past it was nothing for the kings to have 20 or 30 children. The late king had four wives but the present one has only one and is encouraging other people to do the same. In the palace there was no furniture but the most elaborate mosaics everywhere. The walls, pillars and ceilings had no other decorations, all in coloured woods and marble. It almost became monotonous with various patterns repeated only in different colours. The mosaics must have taken many hours to complete, as each piece was small. There were no windows but square holes in the walls. The climate being hot, glass was not required, but in some rooms was a fireplace for chilly nights, when they had low temperatures in winter.

We had a choice to leave the coach and look around the famous Djemaa el-Fna square, or look round the royal tombs (Saadiens tombs). These tombs were in a narrow back street and very old. One area was for children, with a plain oblong slab marking the tomb slightly raised from the floor with a shaped strip of marble, the names in Arabic on the side or on the wall. There were 20 or 30 inside this shelter. Adjoining this were the kings, in the same setting as the children but in a separate room. The roof, walls and pillars were full of mosaics.

We then walked to the local bazaar; in there were hand-crafted gifts especially for the tourists. First we were taken upstairs to see the beautiful carpets, all being made on the premises; one working there was one of our guide's two wives! The carpets had very intricate patterns and they were not repeated. There were hundreds, both folded and hanging on the walls. They could be made as large as required or as small as a doormat. They were costly; no doubt the money went into the owners' pockets and not the workers'. There was a custom to give prospective customers mint tea to drink. You could smell it as soon as you entered a building! It was very cooling.

On the lower floor was handmade furniture, most of it beautifully inlaid with marble or ivory. Many large blanket boxes of different designs were on show. Full-size dining tables, coffee tables, stools, cabinets and ornaments were all adorned with mosaics.

Brass and silverware were in another section; these were mostly jugs and teapots in Moroccan shapes. There were some round pots with lids about four inches across and two inches high; not sure what they were for! Shelves were full of various ceramics, different shapes and sizes. Leather is another product of Morocco; shoes had a sole and front, but the toes ended in a long flat point, not turned up. They looked quite comfortable. Handbags had very decorative designs in the leather. I purchased one of these for approximately £10, but must admit after using it at home for a short period found they were not as perfect as I thought.

As we walked outside the souk men and women were trying to sell us various articles in the street. Almost next to the souk we had been in was a pharmacy, but not exactly as we would find in England. As a group we were invited to sit on the benches provided; they had various types of natural spices, and also potions with strong smells. They were advising different types of herbs for headaches, skin problems, stomach upsets, perfumes and plain spices to cook with food, not only to enhance the flavour but for health. Apparently some spices were to keep one in good health; after seeing some food shops it is no wonder they were required! Still, perhaps one bug helps to kill another! The only thing that interested me was the perfume of orange flower; it really had a sweet smell.

Now we returned to the coach and in a short time we were in the main square. As we had not been allowed to take food into the country we were beginning to feel hungry. Abdel advised us to go to the hotel; it was the only one in the square in the centre of the city. We went there and were greeted and taken inside, into the cool, as by now the temperature had reached 27°C. There was a centre courtyard with gazebos and marble tiles on the floor, covered with beautiful carpets. The decor was in rich colours, with a maroon tablecloth and another white one on top in the centre. I had asked two women if I could join them before we went in. We sat down and two more men from our party joined us. We were not sure what food to taste, but the waiter suggested couscous with lamb, date and raisins. To start with he brought four different plates all containing a spice of some description: one was cold potato, the second was an overcooked cabbage with a bitter taste – it looked the colour of curry – and the last spiced beetroot; I ate most of this myself as the others did not like it! We decided that a bottle of Coca-Cola or water was the safest to drink.

Our lamb arrived beautifully presented, under a sauce of raisin and date; this was made more like a sweet and sour sauce; couscous was around the edge of the plate. I really enjoyed this, as the lamb was so tender and tasty. This was followed by fresh sliced melon and fresh strawberries. After eating it was time to pay; I did not have sufficient dirham, so paid in American dollars. One of the men also was short of dirham, so I lent him money until we returned to the coach. Not a usual topic, but we visited the hotel loo; everywhere you went the doors on both sides were decorated with designs in paint.

We now visited the square to see what was going on; later in the afternoon it was supposed to 'come alive', after the locals had a siesta. The five of us from the lunch table walked round together. I bought some fresh oranges to bring home. I tried to photograph a snake charmer, but he kept standing in front of the snake when it started its dance! He wanted money and I was not prepared to give it to him. Also another man from our party was photographing the snake quite close when the owner demanded money. He refused and two men took either end of the snake and walked up to the photographer. I saw he had problems so shouted to him something about our coach being across the road; the men hurriedly moved away, taking the snake with them. I do not know what they thought I was saying! We had a good laugh when we got back into the coach, where we also settled our finances.

The guide decided to make another stop before leaving. This was an olive grove which had a natural lake with many fish. The water looked decidedly dirty.

Eventually we said our goodbyes to Abdel, and our tour agent took us through customs, going through the passport area, into the waiting room. Although this was a small airport we had to wait an hour and a half. Our guide made enquires and found we were the only aircraft to leave the airport. After some persuasion we were allowed on the craft and took off early. At the airport all aircraft must arrive or take off before dark as there were no lights on the runway!

On the way back the captain had permission to fly at 35,000 feet instead of 33,000 feet, we went into a jet stream and arrived an hour early. Another interesting day, but not keen to go back.

Krakow and Auschwitz
June 2001
(day trip)

When arriving at Bournemouth airport we were told we would be late leaving in order to fit in a flying slot; in fact we waited an hour. It was the same happy band of staff both to greet us and on board. The flight took just over two hours. On arrival it was dry but puddles lay on the tarmac, an omen for the day!

Three coaches were waiting, each with a Polish guide. Information was narrated as we were driven into the town of Krakow. History included how the boundaries of Poland had been changed many times, before the final fixture. As we know the Germans took over in 1939 and in 1945 the country was liberated by the Russians. The country became Communist until 1989. The Russians plundered the country and took everything they could remove, some of it pertaining to the war.

There are now 70 different religions, but the Catholic being the strongest, and the country contains 76,000 monks and priests, plus 26,000 nuns. There are 100 churches in the town; while touring around we passed many.

The first stop was to visit the courtyard of the palace; there are no royal members now, but the place is kept as a museum. It is three storeys high with balconies on each floor. The third floor and a band about three feet from the ceiling had beautiful paintings and mosaic all the way round. It started to rain while we were here, so up went the umbrellas! The palace joined the cathedral, which had domes; one had a gold roof but no gold figures or sculpture.

We looked inside the cathedral and were surprised to find it so dark and sombre; the only light shone on tombs or the altars, with just two chandeliers in the nave. Another thing was surprising as I did not see any stations of the cross, which are in English Catholic churches. The altar surrounds were either in gold or silver. The main altar had enormous pillars up to the roof. Cherubs, also in gold, were displayed close to the roof. There were only two stained-glass windows in the whole cathedral. Two large tapestries had been hung in the entrance of the church but as the light was bad it was not possible to note the full beauty. Pope Paul II was taught within these walls by the priests; he actually took his first mass here; he also returned here and said mass on more than one occasion while Pope. We understood part of the palace had been destroyed and a large garden installed in its place. After the war the buildings and the wall surrounding the cathedral were repaired; benefactors had their names placed on stones in this wall.

As we walked back towards the main square we peered through a hole in the wall and saw the house where Schindler had lived. As we know he saved many Jews by taking them with his factory to Czechoslovakia. I digress slightly because when I was a child some bombs were dropped in a field close to our home during the war. They did not explode and when the soldiers came to dismantle them there was a note inside them saying 'With love from the Czechs'. I can see now they probably came from Schindler's factory.

Many buildings in the town belonged to the church or bishops. One bishop had lived in a house built in the sixteenth century. One street we walked through had buskers playing the most delightful Mozart on bassoon and clarinet; it sounded so perfect for the architecture around them. Also beside them was a student carving images out of wood under a tree.

On our way to where we had to join the coaches later, we were given free time to take a tour round. We found somewhere to eat as time was marching on. We had foot and mouth still in England so had not been able to bring anything with us to eat. We looked round a group of shops before deciding what to eat; we only needed a snack, so I ended up with a fresh bread roll and a choice of several cheeses. There were many tempting cakes for sale but I resisted them! The food was cheap compared with England. A group of us sat together in the square watching the pigeons come and beg for bits. While we ate the snack a small band came close by, busking their country songs and dances. The accordionist was very nimble with his fingers; I could have continued to listen for hours but the time marched on.

The cloth hall was the next venue, so called as they originally wove cloth there and now had stalls with gifts for tourists. This was definitely designed to attract tourists with masses of wooden toys, ornaments, glass of all types and colours, some painted, and dolls in national costume. There were children's waistcoats, in very colourful designs. One stall had sheep and goat skins for rugs and waistcoats for adults. Jewellery of all shapes and sizes with amber and silver. Just outside the hall were artists showing their various pictures in several different modes.

We next met up with the remainder of the tour outside St Mary's church at two minutes to three. As the clock struck the time a trumpeter appeared at a window and played a phrase of music, and repeated this on all four sides of the tower as this was traditional. Another ten minutes' walk and we mounted the coaches, as they were not allowed in the square. There were trams and very few buses and or cars.

The main road seemed to have more lorries than cars. We drove 49 miles out to Auschwitz, or Oswiecim as the Polish prefer to call the place. En route we noticed that garages were selling petrol for approximately 61 pence per litre. The main road out of Krakow had a badly patched surface. There were one or two motorways and more being made. We travelled on one for 11 kilometres and the driver had to pay a toll of about £5. An hour and a half and we reached the first of the Auschwitz camps.

As we had travelled along, smallholders had been farming their crops in strips across the fields with different crops in each strip. They all grew potatoes, some had rye and wheat, many had cut grass for hay as many farms had their house cow and/or a horse. The farm houses were small and mostly built of breeze blocks; these had probably been built since the war. They probably could not afford a facing to the houses as they were very poor. The Russians left the country 12 years prior, plundering all they could. Germans did this also in 1945, so Poland had been left a poor country A large amount of woodland and grass was allowed to grow wild. The population had been greatly reduced through the war.

On arrival at the first camp, the atmosphere was difficult to describe; it was not ghostly, but a very sombre feeling, almost as though one was being watched. We were told all the time the camp was used, leaves did not appear on the trees and there were never any birds. I saw one or two swallows but that was all while I was there. The lime trees planted had their leaves shimmer and move but there was no wind to actually move them. The leaves sounded like running water. A smell was within the camp, but it was not possible to say what it was; it hung in the air; this also applied to any buildings we entered. I felt I could not take photographs inside buildings; it was like trespassing. Some did but I could not; it was too much for me.

Our guide was a young man in his twenties, named Sebastian. He told us his grandfather had been in the camp and he had tried to trace the records to see what had happened to him. He had eventually found his grandfather had been shot. I noticed a couple in our party went to the place where prisoners were shot and laid flowers, for a family member, and then returned in tears.

As the result of sifting through so much information to trace his grandfather, Sebastian felt he had to act as a guide to tell people of the atrocities so as to try and avoid it happening again. I noticed at the end he seemed exhausted, and he said he always feels exhausted at the end of a tour owing to the implications and what he relives. Apparently the Germans left the camp in a hurry in 1945 and they did not have time to destroy all the documents and incriminating evidence, so everything left behind has made it easier to turn the camp into a museum, and to trace relatives of the prisoners or vice versa.

In the roadways were small pillboxes where a guard could stand in bad weather to count the prisoners when roll call was required. We were taken to the Gestapo buildings where their offices were and into the cellars and the various rooms where people were placed. If one man was charged with something as simple as pulling a face at the Gestapo, they would take not only him but his friends for punishment as the friends should have told the Gestapo what he had done. One room had a heavy door; the

154

room was filled with as many humans as possible squeezed in and the door shut. There was no air going in so they all suffocated. In a second room they were locked in and starved to death. There was a little place the size of a telephone box, bricked to the ceiling with just a small door at the base. Men were made to crawl inside and remain standing all night after a day's work, repeating this treatment until they just died. After each day's work they just become weaker and weaker. There were one and a half million who died in this camp.

In another building were remnants, a room full of children's shoes, another with men's, and a further one with women's. Another room showed artificial limbs and back supports; yet another had two tons of human hair. This is what was left; someone managed to photograph hair being bagged like wool fleece and woven into carpets. Cases in which people brought their belongings were displayed in a room with many of the people's names written on them. A certain amount of clothes worn were exhibited. This was all so very heartbreaking to see. We were shown where men and women were separated, also children from the women. The women were of little use to the Germans.

Most of the Jews were enticed into the camps with the promise of a shower and food, particularly the women and children. This was after travelling days in cattle trucks. This unfortunately was the German method of getting them to the gas chamber without too many struggles. They thought they would be having a shower. The showers were tablets of poison dropped through holes in the roof; when made wet they gave off a gas which killed everyone. There were large ovens adjoining the gas chamber where most of the bodies were burnt. Prisoners had the job of doing this.

Electric fences surrounded the place; they were still there for all to see. There were two fences approximately six feet apart and ten or eleven feet high; both were electrified. The wire was strung horizontally every few inches, and occasionally criss-crossed vertically with more wires. A considerable number of people committed suicide on the fences; the guards had lookouts built high to watch the fences for these people, and also escapees.

From this camp we were taken to camp number two. This camp in 1945 was in the process of being enlarged to double its size. The foundations had been laid showing the outlines for the new huts, and a new gas chamber. We arrived to be faced by the famous railway and arch where prisoners walked from the cattle trucks completely full of people. Everyone was put into groups according to their abilities. Old men, children and women were to be the first in the gas chambers, and were treated the same as the people in the first camp. Men were selected for one side of the arch and the women the other. We entered the huts; one showed the beds the prisoners had to sleep on. They were insufficient for the number of people and they slept on top of one another.

One hut was used for latrines; the prisoners were only allowed two visits a day, morning and evening, hence the huts were in a terrible state especially with illness. It was from these huts people were liberated; those who were involved in freeing the prisoners stated they were mentally as well as physically ill. The third camp was destroyed by the Germans before the liberation.

We were told that for a radius of 40 kilometres from the camp all Polish people were removed. Houses were occupied by Gestapo and staff or destroyed. The commandant of the camp, Rudolf Höss, actually lived on the perimeter of the camp with his children. He was tried in Warsaw and hanged in the grounds of the camp. This of course could not bring back all the people killed. In the first camp we saw letters written by Hitler to kill and destroy, destroy, destroy all Jews, and more than 3 million of those killed were Polish.

What can anyone say at the end of this tour? We went back to the airport with most people very subdued on the way home after what we had seen and heard.

I cannot say this was a lovely trip but it was one I felt necessary, very thought provoking with the Auschwitz camp, a tour I will never ever forget, and one I shall never repeat.

Top and bottom: the main entrances to the two camps

Canada
August 2001
(one week)

I had a taxi direct from home to Gatwick airport; it was early travelling, but one had to be prepared for the unforeseen. Time soon passed when Rosemary and I booked in. The flying time to Toronto was seven and a quarter hours; we left at midday and arrived at 3.15pm local time. A gentleman sat next to us en route and told us of different restaurants that provided good food. On landing we had a visa card to complete, and on it was declared that we must not visit zoos, farms or anything to do with animals owing to the foot and mouth back home. We walked on disinfectant mats as a precaution.

A people carrier met us at Toronto airport with an English driver. He had lived in Canada for more than ten years, but still kept his accent. The driver gave us a commentary as we drove through parts of the city. There were one-way streets which took us a long way round to the hotel. After settling in we walked the streets close by, to try and purchase a snack for the following day. The first evening meal we ate at the hotel restaurant, not that we wanted much after the meals on the flight. I telephoned my cousin Gordon who live on the outskirts of Toronto, to say we had arrived.

The next day, Tuesday August 14, Rosemary had breakfast in our room while I went down to a cooked breakfast. Food prices were cheaper than in England. I telephoned Kathy, Gordon's wife, to check when we would meet, and also which day. We went out at 9am only to find the shops and banks did not open until 10am. We had few Canadian dollars! We just wandered round comparing prices in the shops to our own. Some shops had sales but we only bought a few gifts to take home. There were two large shopping complexes, Bay Street and the smaller one at Eaton Centre. We did notice several traders selling side by side with the same goods. At the end of the tour of the various shops our feet decided a rest was required and a few postcards were written.

There was quite a distance to walk to a restaurant which had been recommended for the evening meal. The whole meal cost £7 each. On the way back we walked to and fro along various streets to look round the area. Shops were open much later than at home. We did find one or two little gifts, and arrived back at the hotel in time to receive a telephone call from my cousin. The next day we were to travel by subway to meet the family.

The morning came; it was now August 15. We seemed to have gone through our money quickly, so off to the bank before we did anything else! Now onto the subway to Pickering, a suburb of Toronto. We travelled just underground and found miles of shops underground, most unexpected! I met Kathy, Gordon's wife, at the station; she took us to meet her daughter and her three-month-old grandchild.

We went for a light meal before going to their home. They have such a beautiful home, very spacious, and an entrance hall with a marble floor. My cousin Gordon, who I had last met in 1948, had polio at an earlier age, and now he was in his eighties confined to a wheelchair. He said he had another bout of polio 18 months previous to our visit. We received such a welcome; so nice to see him and meet the family. Kathy and Gordon live comfortably in their son and daughter-in-law's house, along with their son's three children. I had never seen three generations get on together so well. They spent much of their spare time with church matters, Gordon having been the secretary for the church. There was a basement in the house, so when winter came the children had somewhere to play out of the bad weather.

Lori the daughter prepared a delicious roast meal; we all took hands and said grace before starting to eat. The beef was so tender, and it was accompanied by many vegetables and Yorkshire pudding. The desert was profiteroles, followed by coffee. It is a meal I cannot forget with my cousin.

159

Gordon, Kathy and self

The next day it was back to the holiday after experiencing an enjoyable visit to some of my family. We found a type of supermarket which sold some cooked meals, all for 'take away', curries, hot pots and salads. We decided to buy some food for a picnic from here, also including some Danish pastries.

We bought tickets for an on-off city bus. There were 20 different stops on the route, and we were told about the longest road in Canada, called Yonge Street, which covered over a thousand miles. It would have been lovely to see some of the countryside, but foot and mouth back home stopped us. A full commentary was given while we travelled on this red double-decker London bus. The first stop was at Casa Loma, a building built in the style of a Spanish castle. The owner, formerly an Englishman, had grand ideas and started to build the castle, but unfortunately, having expensive tastes, he ran out of money in the 1920s, and only three quarters had been completed. Toronto City Council had since taken over the property. In the main hall we were given mobile tapes, which described every room as we passed through, including the paintings on the walls. The conservatory was very large and contained some lovely hothouse plants. The floor was designed with mosaic tiles, the roof sufficiently high to accommodate some trees. Wood panelling was a feature of the whole house, including the entrance hall. There were two organs, one in the entrance hall and the other on the first floor. A swimming pool had been dug out in the basement but not completed, owing to finances. There was a tunnel which led to the stables and carriage hall. There were many rooms connected to the stables, for the grooms, food and tack. The stalls for the horses were of mahogany with beautiful Spanish tile floors. In a museum there were six or seven different types of horse-drawn vehicles, back to the 1890s.

By the time we had seen all this and the six-acre gardens it had turned to rain. Our tour continued passing places of interest, stopping for the passengers to mount or dismount the bus. Our next stop was the CN Tower, the highest free-standing tower in the world at the time. This has since been superseded. It is 1,815 feet high. It cost tourists £7 to go to the top. We had to queue to take the lift up; it takes 40 seconds to travel to the viewing platform, a terrific panorama over the city to Lake Ontario. I walked on the famous glass floor, where you can see to the ground. Until the tower was built there was poor reception for radio and television. This tower was completed and opened in 1976; the builder wished to demonstrate the strength of a single standing building. It took 40 months to complete, working five days a week. It contains the longest metal staircase in the world. The tower is now classified as one of the seven wonders of the modern world by the American Society of Civil Engineers, standing at 144 floors high.

When we returned to ground level there was a shop with all types of souvenirs. It was time to catch the bus back to the hotel; a tourist bus was due every ten minutes, but we waited and waited and waited. An hour later, after trying to telephone the office, we had started to walk to the railway station when a bus arrived! It was the same person who had taken us on the tour earlier. Rosemary complained about the wait in the rain. The driver was full of apologies, but said the traffic was atrocious as it was a bank holiday. Although the bus should have terminated at the bus station, the driver felt sorry for us and took us back to the hotel. Neither of us wanted rocking to sleep!

The next day was a Friday. One more walk around the shopping mall where the shop had a sale, lucky this time! Rosemary and I only spent a few dollars. The hotel ran a shuttle service to Niagara later in the morning; it took over an hour along Lake Ontario. Niagara is like Brighton by the sea: an area of noise, bingo, houses of horrors and cheap souvenirs. Our evening meal was in a hotel overlooking the falls. We had a window seat 12 floors up; as it got dark the falls were all lit up. There was a special buffet; it was supposed to be the longest buffet table in the world, and we could eat as much as we liked.

After the meal we went down two floors to some comfortable armchairs facing the falls, as the firework display was timed for 10pm over the Canadian part of the falls. There are two different sections of the falls, Canadian and American. We eventually made our way to the esplanade, as did many other people. The actual firework display took ten minutes and cost $25,000. The display takes place every Friday and Sunday evening during the summer months.

The next day a mistake was made regarding where we should catch the bus to see places of interest. We arrived at the Sheraton hotel, and returned to our hotel after waiting an hour. A car took us to catch up with the bus; in fact we had not missed anything as they were still picking up passengers from other hotels! The first stop was at the Carmelite Monastery; monks were no longer in residence although the place was old. It had been used for training purposes in the past. The church looked quite modern inside; one of the priests in charge spoke about the origins of the place.

After this visit the bus drove us along the side of the river; the driver told us to watch out for interesting points along the route. The rainbow bridge, so called owing to its shape, was mentioned as it was the main bridge into America from Niagara. A visa had to be acquired to go over the bridge and this cost approximately £7. It was possible to walk or travel by a vehicle. The driver pointed out where the falls had moved upriver due to erosion, over six miles over 2000 years. The falls now move back one foot every ten years.

One place where a sharp bend is in the river the water comes downstream too quickly for the water to go round the bend; it has formed a whirlpool which covers 68 acres and is 124 feet deep. We got out of the coach to see the whirlpool in the deep gorge.

The next stop was at the horticulture college to see the clock of flowers. There were 20,000 plants, with mechanical workings and even a metal second hand. The college is renowned all over the world for its work, as a place for students to study and as a popular tourist spot.

Top: Niagara Falls (Canadian part). Bottom: at the craft fair in Niagara on the lake.

A dam belonging to the Americans had been built over the river on the lake and generated electricity for many thousands of people. We also noticed an air balloon on the American side, tethered for tourists to go up and see around the area.

We returned to the Canadian falls, got into a lift and travelled 124 feet below ground. At this point we were each given a yellow waterproof cape, as it was possible to walk close to the falls. 22,000 gallons of water flowed every minute over the edge; the water was ten feet thick as it fell, with a drop of 176 feet. The Canadian falls were wider than the American falls, 2200 feet wide at the brink. When one walked behind the falls the thickness of the water dulled everything. This was such a fascinating experience, well worth the visit, something I will always remember.

Niagara has a tower called the Skylon Tower, but not as high as the one in Toronto. After seeing this we returned to the falls; Rosemary decided to go aboard the *Maid of the Mist*, a boat that goes as near as possible to the foot of the falls. I stayed behind and watched.

For the evening meal we visited the 'Secret Garden'; this was on the promenade, hidden by pergolas with many plants climbing. The garden looked lovely.

A thunderstorm raged the next morning, including heavy rain. Rosemary was keen to visit the village Niagara on the lake, a few miles north, as she had been told how beautiful it was. I was not particularly interested, it being so wet, but did go with her, travelling by bus, and on arrival it had stopped raining. We spotted a sign, 'Craft Fair', so paddled around on the waterlogged grass and found it very interesting. Some of the 100 stalls had left owing to the rain, but those remaining showed crafts of woodwork, ceramics, paintings, metalwork. The stall owners did not like me filming as they thought it was for the Canadian papers. The craft show was named after Bernard Shaw as he had lived close by.

Village streets were very pretty; even where people lived, there were avenues of trees. The main shopping street had smaller trees and flower beds on both sides of the road. There were wooden seats scattered along the pavements. Shops were individually owned, no supermarkets and large shops, very different to Toronto. Soon the bus was due so back to the hotel.

Rosemary went to have some tax returned on new goods purchased, but was told it would be posted to her, which it was. The shuttle bus returned us to Toronto airport. Everything went smoothly and we arrived safely back in England.

What did I think of the visit to Canada? A super time, a time to remember.

Sicily
June 2002
(day trip)

Unfortunately we had a bad start to the day; Swanwick's air traffic control centre, which controlled the aircraft for the Bournemouth area, had a computer crash. We were due to leave at 7.30am, but it was 10am for take-off. There was another flight for Palmair about to go to Malaga; as they were due to complete their shift at an earlier time, we swapped crews. Palmair allowed us to return two hours later than scheduled! It was possible to complete our tour.

Although late we still had breakfast served on board. We arrived in Sicily at Catania airport. The airport ground was very flat but we could see Mount Etna rising in the background. The soil here appeared very fertile, until we reached the outskirts of the town, then small lava streams came from Mount Etna. Information given stated that it took 350 years for the lava to be fertile enough to grow plant life. Although Etna was the volcano there were 200 small hot spots, which were likely to erupt when Etna came alive. The nearer to Etna the more barren the land was with old streams of lava getting wider and wider. Apparently when in flow it takes one second to cover five metres. On an old stream I found amongst some tufted grass some violets, the only plants around.

Houses became sparse, but still people decided to take the risk and live higher up the mountainside, places where parts of homes were left standing while the remainder had been covered in lava and burnt out from the eruption in 2001. These lava tracks were still black and got wider as they slid down the side of the volcano.

In some places it was possible to dig in the lava for 18 inches into the ground; some places were still too hot to touch a year later.

On the way towards Mount Etna we stopped at a café, and on the opposite side of the road was a souvenir and coffee shop. The coffee shop was saved by the owner pouring cold water through a window at the back, over the lava as it came to the building. You could see where the lava actually came against the wall of the shop. It became a place to see how near it had been to being destroyed. Many people thought the owner was lucky to still be alive. Apparently the local people know when Mount Etna is likely to erupt it gives signals as a warning.

From here we were driven along the coastal side of Mount Etna; this was a really scenic route, looking along the coast and the cliffs. It was possible to see the Italian coast a few miles north at Messina.

Taomino is a little town on the northern side of Etna, on very steep sides of the hill. It is a very pretty place with the main streets running along the contours of the hill. Side streets are very steep with steps up and down. Tables and chairs or stalls were laid out in the steep area when we visited. Residents cater for the tourists in the shops. It is a lovely quaint town.

Several of us visited the amphitheatre which was in a hollow with views along the coast. This theatre was very old, but still used for concerts with new equipment installed. The old stone seats were still in use, and presumably in the olden times for gladiators etc. I guess if the walls that remained could only talk, many stories would be told.

Right at the very top of the rock outside the town was a castle; we stood in wonder as it was built so high and in a very perilous position, knowing it was sitting on the edge of the volcano!

On the way back to the airport, we passed an island in a bay, close to the mainland; the people who owned it in the past had a beautiful large house built, but refused to allow any public to visit. Now it has been turned into a museum, but still the only way to visit is in a boat across the narrow strip of water.

By the time we arrived for the flight home it was almost dark. It took two and a quarter hours to reach Bournemouth airport.

Yes, a very interesting area to visit; I would like to go back to Taomino, and spend more time exploring.

Lisbon, Portugal
June 2002
(day trip)

Having set off at the scheduled flight time from Hurn and had breakfast, we landed after two hours. Like at several small airports a bus collected us from the aircraft to take us to the terminal. We landed early and waited for the Portuguese guides and three coaches to arrive. The guide gave a little history of the country and Lisbon; this had been the capital since the thirteenth century. On the map Portugal looks small, but it is bigger than Holland, Belgium or Danmark. Lisbon was built on seven hills, and the country became a republic in 1910. An earthquake destroyed most of the city in 1755; it was then rebuilt quickly by a marquis.

While being taken from the airport, I noticed many roads had coloured tiles to shore the sides of the roads; some had designs and others just different bright colours. We passed famous buildings where they still have bull fights, but unlike in Spain they are not allowed to kill the animals in the ring, also matadors fight on foot!

We were taken to Edward VII Park, passing avenues of blue jacaranda trees in bloom. A large memorial was erected there in memory of the revolution that took place in 1974, the end of the dictatorial government. Beside the memorial was a special view of a large garden maze.

The city was built beside the River Tagus's estuary, and deals with incoming and outgoing shipments, as the water is sufficiently deep for ships to come in. Olive oil, wine and cork are amongst the main exports. The river is 300 kilometres long and much wider than the River Thames. On the opposite side of the river there stands a large figure of Christ, a duplicate of the one in South America; this one was built in 1964. Portugal was not involved in the 1939–45 war with Germany, as it remained neutral. We visited one of the large towers built to keep watch over the river during previous wars; nearby was a very large monument to King Edward the Sailor.

There are two large bridges over the Tagus; the old bridge was built in 1966, and the new in 1998 built further up the river. Some buildings on the banks of the river are now museums but were originally rope factories. In days of yore this was a very busy port, with tall sailing ships which required many miles of rigging. There were many war ships in the sixteenth century as they were fighting other countries; now it is predominantly fishing boats.

The patron saint of Lisbon is St Anthony. We went to a monastery church which was absolutely beautiful; I could have spent hours there as it was so interesting. Inside were gorgeous paintings, and chapels, silver work, carvings; these were all worth a special visit. This was such a contrast to the very plain cathedral at the other end of the city, although both were built in a similar period. Getting to the cathedral involved climbing hills, which were steep and had cobbled roads. I found a quick way back via narrow lanes with many steps.

We had spare time for lunch, so walked into the main shopping precinct; in the middle were tables and chairs with parasols, not unlike Paris. Waiters and waitresses came out with the food. Even McDonald's had a place selling ice cream and soft drinks. The price of food was comparable to the English. The temperature while in Lisbon was in the 80s.

After this I spent time just window shopping in the main street. Trams were a popular form of transport. Several of our party went to the castle travelling on one, instead of climbing the hills. It was a spectacular view from the old castle overlooking the area. In a street adjoining the castle was the police headquarters; they all carried guns. Many were on duty walking in the streets in pairs.

General thoughts on the city: the streets were very clean, but very uneven pavements. Some houses and premises were in poor condition, and could be improved with a coat of paint, but a lovely day out. It was an intriguing city, and I would like to go back for a closer look. Coaches took us back to the airport and then the flight home.

Moscow
May 2003
(weekend visit)

An extra early start from Hurn airport, 4am, owing to the difference in the time between England and Moscow. We travelled in a jumbo aircraft with 427 on board. The route to Moscow was over Dover, through Belgium and via Poland. I think we were all half asleep over breakfast! The actual flight took three hours and ten minutes to Domodedovo airport; this was not the main airport for the city. Unfortunately one of the group was taken ill and collapsed on arrival; he joined us later in the day.

It took an hour to get through passport control; the staff had a computer but every small detail had to be put in. We were told before landing not to laugh at any of the staff; this would not be taken kindly! When we landed there was a very sombre attitude. Now we had noticed the speed of working; regardless of anything, it was all one speed: 'slow'. This was the speed for the weekend! Jenny and I eventually boarded coach eight; there were ten.

The guide with us was called Val, a shortened version of a male Valerie. He spoke good English, which he had learnt in Moscow; I think also his knowledge of English had improved when we left! We spoke to him during the tour; he had had to study hard in various subjects to pass many examinations before qualifying as a guide. Two of his favourite phrases were 'You know' and 'OK'. The trip from the airport took an hour and he talked the whole time about Russia and Moscow, giving history as well as up-to-date information. He mentioned that there were police in uniform, also there were as many in plain clothes and they would be watching us.

In the sixteenth century many of the females of the royal family were put in convents, particularly if there were squabbles within the family, years ago many females who did not marry were also sent to a convent to take the veil and become a nun. Peter the Great put his own sister Sophie into a convent after a squabble and there she remained for the rest of her life. There were 21 convents at the time of our visit; if people were homeless, they were sent to a convent or to a monastery as monks, an easy way out of poverty.

The city of Moscow was formed in 1147, as a small town, Kiev, was the original capital of Russia. Russia is one of the richest countries in the world, with 33% of the world's diamonds, and gems, marble and other useful minerals can be found in the Ural Mountains, but it has some of the poorest people. At the moment the situation is one of getting used to the new way of life; after communist ruling, many people do not understand business or how to go about it. In the past they were told what to do and not allowed to think for themselves. Crime is low; the people are probably too frightened not to obey the rules owing to the consequences. They have not forgotten the way the communists treated them for misdemeanours.

Moscow as the new capital is 110 miles round the outskirts and ringed by a motorway not unlike the M25 that surrounds London. The residents drive on the opposite side of the road to the English. There are 9 million people living in the city. No houses were built just for one family before 1917. Before 2002 when President Putin signed the Treaty of Moscow no land had been owned privately, and people could not travel from one village to another or town to town. In the 1930s there were small pieces of land worked by individuals, but they did not own the land; buildings were built for them but no houses in which to live. When communism changed in 1993, people were given a small piece of land on which they worked and had summer houses, or dacha. It was only during the last 12 years that the government started to build homes on the outskirts of Moscow; they were mostly flats, but private owners were allowed to build houses on small pieces of ground. No mortgages are allowed in the country;

if people wish to save to buy, they are unable to bank their money. A flat would cost the equivalent of £24,000 and this would probably only have one bedroom. At present the currency is roubles and one rouble equals two pence in English money.

There are less than 1% unemployed; no wonder we saw three or four women in a line working, sweeping the pavements with long-handled brushes and dustpans. The pension for the elderly is 80 American dollars per month. Rent for a flat is three dollars a week for the pensioners.

Towns and villages were reverting back to names from before the communists had taken over. For example Leningrad had gone back to St Petersburg; streets that had communist names had also been changed. The people wanted to forget the difficult times under the government in the past.

On the way to the hotel we came through the city, and stopped to see places of interest. The lake that inspired *Swan Lake*, with the convent Novodevichy in the background. Swans are brought to the lake for the winter months so they can be fed, as the winters are extremely cold. The cemetery of Novodevichy had Russian and Soviet celebrities buried. We were taken to see the burial places of generals, names of whom I had heard, also ballet dancers (male and female), opera singers, writers and poets such as Tolstoy and Pushkin, and past presidents. The graves were very close together and had elaborate headstones. Many flowers were in oval-shaped wreaths, some three or four foot long, and this was regardless of the length of time the person had been buried. One grave set aside was of Gorbachov's wife Raisa. None of the headstones were green so presumably someone spent time keeping them clean. Crowds of visitors were visiting at the same time, and charges were made for entrance to this cemetery.

Sparrow Hills is one of the highest points in Moscow where the city can be viewed. It was here we saw two wedding couples. One couple released doves, and also had a drummer drumming, but we did not know the significance. The brides both wore white gowns and veils, carrying a posy of flowers; the grooms had a white flower in the buttonhole. One or two guests were the worse for drink. The couples had a stretch limousine to take them on their way. The car was decorated with flowers on the front and rear.

Jeremy Spake of TV *Airport* fame was on our coach, along with Paul Clifton for BBC TV South, who was filming the whole trip. It was interesting talking to the two, particularly Jeremy, as he was born in Leningrad and also he could afford a flat in Moscow and his own car. He had come to St Petersburg to see his grandmother before going on assignment in Siberia. Paul told me he would spend the next two days in a dark room when he returned home, and only four or five minutes would be used by the TV.

Further stops were made along the Sofiyskaya embankment, looking over the river Moskva towards the Kremlin, to see the famous Peter the Great monument. This is made of metal and stands over 100 feet high. Peter is standing on a ship with furled sails. In real life Peter the Great stood six feet seven inches tall. He was a very clever man, using his hands for many crafts, making his own clothes, boots, boats and armour. Famous landmarks were pointed out as we passed, where Pushkin, Tolstoy and the Bolshoi Ballet had lived and worked, also some embassies, a few of the 450 churches, five synagogues, 50 free churches. Out of these there are four Catholic churches and nine monasteries, but many are now museums.

Public transport was mostly used, as it was cheap, although there were many cars within the city, the main problem being parking. Buses, trams and the metro were the most common modes of transport. At one petrol station, the price of petrol was similar to that in present-day England. On the metro it was possible to travel the whole day for the equivalent of pence.

Eventually we arrived at our hotel Rossiya; it was 7pm (Russian time) and we booked into the rooms. The hotel took our passports, and would return them when we left. (They probably did not want us to escape!) When we opened the bedroom door it was hot, 30°C; luckily the windows were open. Our room was en suite with two single beds, which were very comfortable, but no time to stop as Val was taking us to find food to eat near Red Square, which was a reasonable price. There was a long line of various types of food, but it was not as hoped. Another person from our coach joined us but we did not find anywhere suitable. I did not fancy the chicken thighs with some intestines wrapped inside. There were vegetarian meals. Neither of us ate much. The cost was £1.25 each; they weighed their food and we paid accordingly. We found another place that sold ice creams; they were very pleasant flavours, and sold for approximately 16 pence. After this experience we walked back through Red Square to the hotel. Each time we went to our room a porter stood at the bottom of the stairs, checking our identity. I think this could well be used in English hotels. When we went to bed the temperature was still 26°C. Some dogs spent most of the night howling!

It was a treat to have a shower after a hot sticky night. Breakfast was self-service, with plenty of fruit juice, dry bread rolls and sliced luncheon meat, cheese, jam and marmalade. A semi-hot meal could be chosen with sweet potato cakes, omelette and meat, coffee or tea. We had been given the executive bedrooms; before leaving home we had been told the accommodation was 1960s. Five coaches left for the Kremlin. While waiting I saw the BBC reporter Brian Hanrahan come to the hotel.

We were taken round to the other side of the Kremlin to enter. The Kremlin is mostly fifteenth-century; it was originally built in white limestone, but in 1864 new buildings were built in red brick. No one has lived there since the communists took over in 1917, but it all belongs to the leader of the country. Back in history there was a siege and 199 cannons that were in the area were left behind when the army made a hurried retreat. The main building is used for special occasions with banquets for the head of state; the newest one is built of concrete, is used for concerts and conferences and really looks ultra-modern. A Russian film seminar was taking place that day. Other building were where well-known personalities from history lived and are now state offices. There are many churches inside, with onion-shaped domes; some are museums. One had a carillon of bells, which still played. One extra-large bell had never been hung and still remained on the ground. A small park was within the Kremlin and had trees and flower beds.

Another small inner square contained three churches; one was used for christenings, another for marriages, and the third for burials. We went in the third church where the walls were covered in mosaics. No chairs; the congregation had to stand for the service, which could last up to two hours. I do not think I could stand that long! Famous people had come to this church for burial. Apparently Ivan the Terrible was refused entry into the church; he was not liked or trusted, or thought to be religious.

We walked a little further down the road to the armoury, also within the walls. Despite the name it contained artefacts from the past. We asked how they were able to remain as much of the past had been destroyed by the communists; apparently they had just sealed the place, and left it complete. Many clothes made for church clerics were very heavily embroidered with gold and silver thread, or pearls from the local river; these were very old. Also included were other garments with jewels; these vestments weighed as much as 24 to 36 kilos; the headgear was also very heavy and included many different jewels and was now beyond price!

One part had various wedding gowns from queens over a period of time. These were also very highly embroidered and had many expensive jewels. Several dresses were for 14-year-old brides. Peter the Great married twice and both dresses were on show. It was said the wives never wore a dress more than once. Many of the jewelled crowns were worn for special occasions, and had a fur base to make them more comfortable.

The earliest horse-drawn carriage on view dated back to the fourteenth century and had velvet drapes; it was used for royalty. There were no springs and the cart tracks could be very rough, so it was not uncommon for staff to lift the wheels out of the ruts. Later carriages and sledges for nobility were on show and they had springs to make them more comfortable. One sledge was made of leather and totally enclosed. The coronation coach was covered in gold, but very heavy for the horses to pull.

There were many floors of exhibits, which need to be seen to be appreciated. There was china; there were gold and silver platters, chalices, jewelled book covers, and icons of people; much of this also went back to the fourteenth century. All items were too valuable to place any financial value on. One section had human armour and also some horse armour for going to war. It would have been possible to spend so much more time to study the craft and beauty of the work. It is beyond my comprehension how the communists managed to leave all this untouched!

After this it was back to the twenty-first century! The coach took us a short distance to a shopping precinct to find lunch and also see stalls in Old Arbat Street; we had free time to wander round. Three of us went to an Italian restaurant and enjoyed pizza that had a lovely thin base. Mine was cheese and ham, but the ham was actually bacon. Other restaurants did not look so appealing, so it was better to be safe! There were not many stalls in the street, and those there seemed to be selling the same types of articles. I did manage to haggle and bought a set of the 'tumble' dolls for £2.

We met up again with Val and took a short walk to the metro, 94 metres down an escalator to a platform. Everywhere was so clean, with polished marble floors, and even down each side of the escalator was polished. One of our group said it looked more like a ballroom! The trains ran every two minutes and a sign told you how long you would wait for the next one. If drivers were late they were financially penalised. After trains left the station they increased speed quickly and I was sure they were much faster than the English. It was an interesting visit with such lovely surroundings, no graffiti, chandeliers hung from some ceilings and paintings and murals at each end of the platforms. One station had paintings on the ceilings; there were more than 12 on one platform. Each of the six stations we saw was different, other than the marble polished floors. Our final stop was in Red Square. The metro has 165 stations. England is a long way from the cleanliness, speed and cheapness. This was quite an eye opener!

Once again we were left with free time to shop in 'GUM'. During the communists' time the shops all belonged to the government, but now they were individually owned. Clothes were about the same price as England, and sold in places similar to our shopping malls. We also had time to walk through 'Red Square' taking photographs of the tomb of Lenin, with the background of the Kremlin wall. We were not able to go inside as he was being re-embalmed. St Basil's Cathedral stood in front of our hotel. It had been a hot day so we were hoping to find some seats for a rest. No matter where you looked there were no seats outside.

After coffee we waited for the coaches, but were told by a guide that the aircraft that brought us had been to Paris since, and was in the Bahamas taking President Chirac there. Our aircraft home was coming from Chicago after a service, taking a load to Manchester before coming to Moscow. Unfortunately there had been engine trouble and the plane was not due to arrive for a further two hours. The only place we could find to sit was a café in the hotel. At least we enjoyed some fruit and ice cream while waiting. This cost us about £1.20.

Finally we returned to Domodedovo airport; unfortunately when we came to board six people had drunk too much and were left behind. I eventually arrived home at 1.55 am. It was Monday morning and I was absolutely shattered! Over the two days we had walked for approximately for ten hours.

My thoughts on the trip! The people were more modern than anticipated and the young wore brightly coloured clothes. It appeared that only the elderly wore black clothes and looked drab. Cars of all sizes were prolific; there must be more money than when the communists ruled. This was a very enjoyable tour, which educated us regarding modern life in Russia.

St Basil's Cathedral

Kobenhavn and Memories
August 2003
(day trip)

This was not my first trip to the capital of Danmark, but a visit after several years' break. The airport had been enlarged to two terminals, whereas on the first visit there was only one small one which contained one long corridor and the building was of prefabricated material, more like a Nissen hut with various gate numbers. The staff used to have scooters to travel up and down the corridor, although this time on the way home some staff still used them.

At least it was quick checking through all the passengers, with their passports. The customs officer and I had a joke in Danish, as I speak the language. For this tour we had a double-decker bus and a single coach to take us round to various places of interest. Kastrup the airport, like airports in many other countries, was some way outside the city and on a separate island. The first impression even before landing was that Danmark is well advanced with wind turbines. There were some close to the Storstrom bridge, and also three other groups not far from land.

There is a new bridge and tunnel from Kastrup to Sweden; the bridge could be seen from just outside the airport although some distance away. Apparently it is quite easy coming out of the airport to take the wrong turning and end up in Sweden!

We had an English-speaking guide who was a jolly person and gave details about the history of the country. There had been seven wars in which the country had been involved over a period of time, but mostly with Sweden and Germany. During the 1939–45 war Germany overran Danmark. I was told about this while working in Lolland back in 1957/58. It was not until I was working there that my employer's father was put in prison as he favoured the Germans; Lolland was only 20 minutes from the coast of Germany.

Tales were told where a van load of bread from the bakery also contained a dead pig in between the loaves, so the Germans could not see the meat. People were very strictly rationed for food during this period. Farmers were better off as they could grow their own vegetables, and then an odd pig or calf died!

Back to the tour: we were taken past the retirement houses of sailors who had left the sea. One king had the rows of houses built in recognition of their service at sea. The houses are still painted in the old mustard colour. Statues were along our route and we were told who they represented, or were dedicated to.

The English church St Alban's still looked the same; I had worshipped in there when in Kobenhavn. Years ago when showing cattle at a royal agriculture show a friend and I had attended morning service. The agriculture show was quite an experience as we were the only two girls and also the only English participants. Dairymen also showed their cattle and got together and brought all the cattle food required for us from the store, so we did not have hard work carrying hay and straw; also they cleared away any manure. We were not sure if this was to impress us or just plain good manners! I admit they gave us a good night out after our 13 prizes had been presented to us!

The first night on the showground we were sleeping in a very small tent. We had a struggle to get settled, then a man's voice outside said, 'Is this the tent I am sleeping in?' He was told no, but it made us giggle after the struggle we had as our toes touched one end and our head the other. The following day we had the prizes presented by the present Queen Margrethe, then only princess. When milking we drew quite a large crowd; not many women milk cows in Danmark. The showground has now been built on with many flats several storeys high.

The Little Mermaid was a must as far as our guide was concerned. Unfortunately, since the first time I had seen the statue, her head had been removed twice. It has now been filled with concrete so it can no longer be removed. The wife of one of the presidents modelled for the head, as the second time it was removed it was badly damaged. Years ago I remembered an old man playing a barrel organ just opposite the statue.

Top: the Little Mermaid. Bottom: a city scene

We made a visit to the Queen's royal palace when the changing of the guard was taking place. In the past I had seen the late queen with her children come out of the palace on bicycles. During the 1939–45 war the Germans asked the king where his guards were; he replied that his people were his guards and protectors. The heir to the throne, Prince Frederik (named after his grandfather), has now married his Australian lady.

Further on we visited Nyhavn; there is a large anchor here to remind people this was a naval area. Today the area is full of restaurants and a recommended place to eat. Back in 1958 it was an area of drunken people and a red light place. We would not have considered visiting the area.

The next stop was the main shopping precinct close to the canals. We boarded a boat and had a trip along the canals and into the harbour, something I had not done in the past. The harbour has changed so much; where all the ship building took place is now a housing estate, with one large building left housing a leisure place and an indoor golf course. The royal yacht was anchored and still used to visit many of the islands with the Queen on board. There are over 160 islands so the yacht is useful. It is very elaborately painted.

After the boat trip I left the rest of the party and went my own way, around various streets and shops bringing back memories. The shopping street seemed to have got longer since the 1950s. The Kobenhavn fisherwomen have left their spot on the canal, except for one who now has a gazebo on the side of the canal, but no fish are kept in the canal water. I remember when six or seven women used to sell their fish, keeping them alive in the canal water. I presume it is as it is now because the water is no longer clean enough.

Danmark has not changed financially as it is still more expensive than England, not only for clothes and food but because one is taxed many times over on the same money. On the way home I heard some of the party discussing the cost of a pint of beer, nearly £6 in English money. An ice cream I bought was the equivalent of £2.60, cups of coffee £3. They still use Danish kroner, not euros. At this time there were just over ten kroner to the English pound, but in 1957 I remember getting 19 kroner to the English pound. Things have changed a little!

Radhus Square, the main square in the centre of the city, now has ugly buildings in the middle; years ago it was a clear square for buses and trams to stop. They still make stops there but in a small portion of the square. On the corner of Vesterbrogade the four-storey building is still there; in the past the whole building belonged to the Danish airline SAS. One floor contained a very good restaurant; now each floor has a different airline office:

Thai, Turkish and Chinese. Opposite was a waxwork museum with many effigies inside.

The fisherwomen as they used to be

I took a walk towards the railway station and found the street was full of shops and the little kiosks where cigarettes and daily papers could be bought had all disappeared. The main part of our group had lunch in the Tivoli gardens. There were several differences to the last time I was there. The trees had grown much larger, and all the tents and carts selling hot dogs, ice cream, candyfloss etc. had disappeared, replaced by rows of shops with souvenirs along one side. I think also there were now fewer side shows, ghost trains, houses of horrors etc. There were one or two helter-skelters and high rides instead. The concert hall was there and the second one turned into an outside stage. The lake where the firework displays had been set off had also gone. There was plenty of seating to enjoy the gardens.

The weather this particular day was cloudy and somewhat chilly. In England it had been 36°C. Normal temperatures for the summer months in Danmark were very warm, but very cold winters. When I worked out there we had six weeks of frost, including hoar frost which snapped branches off the top of trees. In the summertime I was helping to make hay in temperatures of 32°C.

Back to the 2003 visit! After our day out the coaches met us and returned us to Kastrup airport; some of us did last-minute shopping. During the journey home I realised I had lost my purse with my card and kroner inside. Our guide tried to help as I knew which stall I had visited and bought something at, but regardless I never heard anything about it.

It was pleasant to visit again, bringing back memories, but to have a holiday there, no thank you! I prefer the memories.

Bratislava
September 2003
(day trip)

We took off on another day trip, with a journey of only one hour 58 minutes. The airport at Bratislava was on the eastern side, so we flew over the city first. We only required two coaches with guides. The coaches were very new and comfortable. Again we heard a little about the place's history. We were only 14 kilometres from the border of Hungary, ten from Austria and seven from the city centre. The trees had an autumn look as they were beginning to change colour. It had been very dry so it was possible they were changing colour early. When we came in to land we noticed all the corn crops had been harvested from the fields.

For 200 years Bratislava was the capital of Hungary and the Danube became the boundary of the country. Eleven Hungarian kings and eight queens were crowned in the city. Bratislava had the very first town park in Europe in 1716, with beautiful trees and places to walk. For 50 years Slovakia was ruled by Russia. Under communist rule many expenses were paid by the state, but now they were paid by residents. The wages for 1969/70 were £36 and now during this visit were an average of only £42 per week. The Russians handed over control to Slovakia in 1969.

We drove past the Volkswagen factory which was originally for Skodas. There were still 15% of the people unemployed and approximately 4% of these were students who were out of work after graduating. There were seven universities and students came from all over the country to attend. The population of Bratislava was 500,000, with the total in Slovakia being 5.3 million. The people are very sport-orientated and there were different stadiums for individual sports, such as basketball, hockey, football, tennis, swimming and athletics; all these stadiums are within one area of the city. By St Martin's Cathedral stands part of an art college and windows in an old building have been painted in a modern style to brighten the place as well as exhibiting the artists' work. St Martin's has a crown on top of the spire; this crown is three feet across, covered by many kilos of gold.

In the city there are 27 churches and many monuments including one as a memorial to the many Jews who were killed in the Holocaust. The Jewish synagogues were demolished during the 1939–45 war, as were several areas where they lived. We saw plaques on some buildings to commemorate Mozart and his last visit to the Conservatoire, also Franz Liszt where he lived and composed some of his music.

Vineyards were on the side of the mountains which were 45 kilometres away. Large quantities of wine are made and exported abroad, not forgetting some is drunk locally. At the time of this visit there was only one brewery left which worked, called Stein; this had been working since 1878, but has since closed.

The tallest building has 35 floors and was built in 1999 for a bank. It is completely self-sufficient with its own electricity and water supply. In the city there are 27 banks, all privately owned. Two new buildings had been built, one like a table upside-down, the other the shape of an inverted pyramid; the modern architecture is not popular with the people. In every square there was a well or fountain, this stemmed from the old days when all buildings were built of wood. The fire risk was always very high.

We passed large villas that were for the aristocracy including one for the president. Not one building was in good repair; outside walls required repairing before a coat of paint. We went to the castle which was 85 metres high on a hill overlooking the Danube river. It was here that so much history had taken place. A separate book could be written on the wars started by religion and jealousy. The outside castle walls are 12 feet thick; even so, cannons fired from across the river caused the old castle to be burnt down. It was a ruin for 150 years, but restored during 1953 to 1968. The dungeon where prisoners had been kept had a deep well. The water was pumped from the mountains from melted snow and was pure and clear. The second floor of the castle is now a museum for the city as records can be traced back to 500 years before Christ. A memorial could be seen from the castle hill, placed 1000 feet high on a mountain east of the city. Two hundred and fifty Russians were buried there in 1969 as a result of trouble with the local people!

At the time of my visit there were three bridges over the Danube in Bratislava and another new one to be built. The old bridge was built in 1819, but it was blown up by the Germans during the 1939–45 war and rebuilt in 1970, having a modern design. On the opposite side of the Danube was a large oil refinery fed directly from the Russian pipelines.

Many streets were pedestrian only, therefore looked a little like Paris with tables, chairs and umbrellas all outside. They were already catering for many nationalities with the cafés. People eat outside until October; when the weather changes they retire to the cellars which are under the normal restaurants.

We went back to the palace as earlier it had been closed for a conference. The rooms inside were enormous and contained paintings and tapestries which had been made in Mortlake, England. These told of Greek mythical legends. The main conference hall was made to look larger with very large mirrors, from floor to ceiling. The town hall was just outside, three storeys high with balconies, and had been established in 1817 but now remained as a museum.

The people of Bratislava had a sense of humour. On one side of the street was a sign in English saying 'Man at work'; under this was an effigy in metal of a man half in a drain, but leaning on his arms on the pavement. Nearly all tourists stopped and looked and of course took photographs! Goods in the shops were very expensive.

In the afternoon our group were taken on a cruise on the Danube to look at the bridges. On landing we were shown how when the river had broken its banks it had flooded on to the land. The water had come down from the mountains after heavy rain and it was too much to be contained within the river. It caused a lot of damage to the town.

When returning to the airport we entered a very large warehouse with goods for retail. It was an interesting exercise comparing the prices of everyday goods. It became dark at 7pm when we went to catch our flight back home. This was an enjoyable day, but not unlike other countries I had visited that had been under a communist regime. It would be nice to visit some of the countryside.

St Petersburg
April 2004
(weekend visit)

Another very early start owing to the time difference; we left England at 6.15am, after the air slot had been agreed. It took three hours and ten minutes, arriving at Pulkovo airport, which was on the outskirts of the town. There was glorious sunshine and no clouds, and this remained for the whole visit.

Three coaches and guides took us round on the tour; this had been arranged back in January. The young Russian guide we had proved to speak very good English and to be very knowledgeable about St Petersburg, imparting some of its history during the two days we were there. We learnt near the end of the tour he was a medical student at one of the universities.

The first impression was that most people looked terribly glum and this remained with us during the tour; wherever we went people lacked smiles, except for our guide Paul. Although many people were around the place was very quiet. Most buildings were in need of repair, but for the museums and palaces; these were extremely ornate, having been painted and renovated. St Petersburg was fairly affluent as cruise ships came in and brought money to the town.

On the drive to Pushkin Palace, milestones or kilometre stones were along the side of the road, standing about six feet tall. These marked every kilometre with numbers on them. St Petersburg had been built on marshland and was actually three metres below the Baltic Sea; consequently water and some snow still lay around. During the Second World War Nazis occupied the city and many deaths took place. The cemetery was very large and contained over a million bodies. Lenin had planned to give the Germans St Petersburg. Siemens, the large German firm, invested a large amount of money into the city industry.

Our first stop was at Pushkin Palace, which had been built for Peter the Great's wife Catherine. Snow still lay on the ground; we waited to be allowed inside. Paul told us in summer months many German and American people came and queues waiting outside were very long. Apparently the two groups would meet up and fights would occur. Police and ambulances would have to be called, and casualties taken to hospital.

The palace was now 300 years old, built in 1703. It had been especially renovated for the 300th anniversary. The outside was blue and white with all decorations and figures in gold. This made the place very impressive before entering. The main gates were wrought iron painted in black and gold. The main building was on one side of the quadrangle. On entering our coats were removed and placed in a cloakroom, which was free of charge, then special plastic slip-overs were given us to place over our shoes to protect the beautiful polished wooden floors.

Inside there appeared to be hundreds of rooms, but some were used very little in the past. Why so many? Each room was highly decorated and contained priceless inlaid furniture and clocks. The ballroom took my breath away when I first entered: the number of decorated mirrors on the walls, plus the paintings on the ceilings; an enormous floor with inlays of different types of wood enhancing the patterns formed. The amber room contained six different types of amber, all in different designs, all so exquisite. Paintings of various sizes were in all rooms, also the ceilings had been painted by various artists. The cost of maintenance for such a place must be horrendous. Paul our guide took us through each room, explaining as we went through. This took us two and a half hours and was worth every minute.

On the way to the Pulkovskaya hotel where we were staying Paul continually talked about various city buildings we passed. Some of the buildings still had the marks left by bullets and explosions from the Nazis. Apparently there were 150,000 bombs dropped on the city during the war. We passed the Triumphal Arch which had been built as a memorial to the victory over the Turkish army in 1828, and also Napoleon was mentioned many times. There were 600 churches before the last war, but now only 400 stood. There is a small artificial canal in the centre; this was made in the nineteenth century. The advocates of abstinence from alcohol were very active in the early twentieth century; they built a church; it was thought this would help the situation.

We were told about the market where hay was sold for the cattle, also firewood and food for the local people. Now it is an ordinary street market. In the year 2000 a tower of peace was built that displayed 300 languages written on the sides.

On arrival at the hotel there was little time to prepare for the evening as a visit to Nikolaevsky Palace had been planned. Outside the palace buskers were playing our national anthem and one or two popular English tunes. A three-course meal had been prearranged and contained a mixed salad with cranberries, caviar and hard-boiled savoury eggs. The main course consisted of dwarf beans, rice, pork and a curdled but tasty sauce. Finally we had pancakes with syrup, and a selection of tea completed the meal.

After the meal we were taken to a theatre for a concert of Cossack dancing, and folk songs were also in the repertoire. One dancer was really outstanding acting like an English clown; a musician played many musical instruments, such as a miniature accordion, a saw, smokers' pipes and a boot. There were many changes of bright costumes. The concert lasted two hours, but the time just flew by. We went out after the concert and buskers were playing on a horn and a bass wind instrument with more English tunes.

After the concert we were taken on a tour to see the lights; actually Moscow had even more lights. It was possible to see ice still floating down the river; the previous week the whole river had been completely frozen. At the time of this visit the population of St Petersburg was 5 million, and it was the second largest town in Russia. We arrived back at the hotel at midnight and neither Jenny nor I took long to get to sleep after a very interesting day.

The next morning we got up early, to a Russian breakfast. I tried to toast a piece of bread in their toaster; it was put in twice and still not brown, just dryer. Scrambled egg was served but cold, but the cold sliced meat was very tasty. Plenty of orange juice was available, but I left Jenny to try the coffee. She eventually decided on the tea! Like Moscow we had to give up our passports on arrival; they were then returned when we signed out from the hotel.

The 'Church of Spilt Blood' was a memorial to Alexander II who had been assassinated on the site. It was completed in 1907 and contains a large amount of mosaic work. The main destination for the day was the Hermitage Museum and Winter Palace. It has seen wars, revolutions, neglect and thefts and has now been restored after an existence of 200 years.

The Nevsky Prospekt street was for shopping or obtaining something to eat.

This was one of the friendliest tours we had been on, and yes I would go again (and indeed have been since).

Salzburg
June 2004
(day trip)

Only just over an hour to fly to Salzburg; we were met by buses at the airport, to take us to the terminal. A good start to the day – raining! This visit we had three coaches all with English-speaking guides. Ours was English but had lived in Austria for several years.

Our guide David kept up a continual patter about the country and some of its history. Austria consisted of nine different areas like our counties. Salzburg was the capital of the largest and had a population of 600,000. It is on the border of Bavaria which is part of Germany. In 1995 the border and customs divide between the two countries was discontinued, and now it is possible to drive freely from one country to the next, without knowing which country you are in!

We were on the way to the 'Eagle's Nest' or 'Kehlsteinhaus'; this was a building built 6017 feet above sea level on the top of a mountain. It took three quarters of an hour to get to the top. Halfway up we came to a level where Hitler, Bormann and Goebbels all had beautiful houses built on the side of the mountain amongst the woodland scenery. The houses have all been pulled down to prevent the public from treating the place as a shrine to these people and making pilgrimages there. Hitler committed suicide in a Berlin bunker and not here as some people thought. It was at this height we changed buses for vehicles with more powerful engines and special brakes for the last four-mile steep climb, and this was where the flora and fauna changed. There were many different types of pines and larch trees; as we climbed there were patches of snow still beside the road.

Top: typical Salzburg scenery. Bottom: another scene.

The lane to the Eagle's Nest had been made from rock which had been blasted or chipped away by hand. Many of the workers had been on duty 24 hours a day. Eight hundred and seventy men became exhausted and every five weeks new men had to be sent there to carry on the work. Accommodation had been built at

Berchtesgaden for the men and their families, and special wages paid. It took 13 months to complete and this included the tunnels where the road passed through. All this was completed for Hitler's fiftieth birthday on April 20 1939, six years after he came to power. The Eagle's Nest was given to him by the German people. The road was built so that it blended into the hillside; it was known Hitler was a keen ecologist and was keen to preserve nature, not people! A fence was finally built round the mountain at 3000 feet from the top, ten miles in length. In this enclosure bird boxes were placed to encourage the birds to breed. During the war bombs were dropped all round the building but not one made a direct hit.

The last 400 feet to the top we were transported in a lift. This was made in brass and mirrors as Hitler suffered from claustrophobia. It only took seconds to rise to the top.

The rooms in the Eagle's Nest have now been turned into restaurants and all money made goes back into the local village. We went into Hitler's lounge where he entertained his dignitaries; it contained a large open Italian fireplace. This had been badly chipped by Americans liberating the building, who had knocked pieces off as mementoes to take home. One story told us was of an American woman who was one of a group of tourists who had specifically come to see the fireplace; she produced a piece from her pocket which her husband (now deceased) had removed from the fireplace and taken home! The outside walls were three feet thick and made of local stone. Many people had wanted the place destroyed, but a local man had saved it as a tourist attraction.

Unfortunately the weather prevented us seeing the view from here as the mountain was covered in mist. We saw photographs of the lovely views.

During the winter frost and snow loosen rocks so each spring the sides of the roads have to be cleared and made safe for tourists. There have not been any accidents since only the special buses have been allowed to the top piece of road since 1952; it is closed to all other vehicles. By the time we reached the base of the mountain the rain had stopped. Most of the river ran beside the road; although not in full spate it ran fast with some rapids.

Salzburg is surrounded by mountains of various heights and is a very attractive place with many narrow lanes, particularly in the older part of the town. We were taken to part of the town and left to explore at will. Jenny and I went to the house where Mozart was born; in some respects I was disappointed as most of the history was written and framed on the walls. We mostly saw pictures, rather than furniture and instruments, although there were two pianos and two violins. We appreciated that the family were very poor so little furniture would have been used. The streets nearby were cobbled and narrow, with some cafés with chairs and tables outside. There was a funicular to take people up to the fortress, but we did not go and investigate.

The cathedral in Salzburg

The 'Dom zu Salzburg' – the cathedral – was worth a visit and had green copper domes. Outside the main doors were two large trees in pots, with more inside. A bishop had come from Ireland to consecrate the first cathedral in 774. This old cathedral was demolished after a bad fire and the present one built in 1628. A bomb destroyed the dome on October 16 1944 and it was repaired and opened again on May 1 1959.

Inside we were surprised by the position of four organs and different-sized pipes. Paintings were high on the ceiling of the dome, and round the walls, including the altar. The carvings at the ends of the pews were very old and had been made before the dome was damaged. Unlike Russia there were no gilt decorations, but it was a very peaceful place to visit.

We stopped for a snack and an apple strudel before returning to the coach. This was a charming town which I would love to visit again, not forgetting the Eagle's Nest on a clear day.

Kerry and Killarney, Ireland
August 2004
(day trip)

Just a short flight to our destination, 58 minutes, and too short for a cooked breakfast, but we received a cup of coffee instead!

Kerry airport was the smallest airport we had travelled to and landed at, so much like Bournemouth in the 1950s. Three coaches were awaiting our arrival. I managed to change my seat on the coach as I was facing the back and I am prone to travel sickness! The weather forecast for the day was 24°C, but instead we had plenty of rain.

View from aircraft between Cork and Kerry

The Irish guide had a very happy-go-lucky attitude, a sense of humour and a beautiful tenor voice. In between stops he would sing some Irish songs and so kept us in a jolly mood. He was very much a family man and we heard all about them.

The southern area of Ireland had had contacts in the past with Australia, some people having been deported in the early 1800s. It is well known that the Irish are superstitious and various tales were told. One story was that one mountain in the Kerry rings was 3414 feet high, but the moon could not climb over the top, so the fairies went up on a dark night and took off one foot, and now that it is only 3413 the moon can climb over! Boys were often given a girl's name to stop the fairies taking them away to work for them; once taken away they were never seen again. In fact our guide's middle name was Mary!

In the south of Ireland there were 8 million sheep, and although this is a large number, lamb is expensive to purchase as most of it is exported to France. One other export is Kerry butter and this is a large industry although not many cattle were seen on this tour. Most fields seem to have beef animals and young stock.

We were driven along the 'motorway' and this was the equivalent of one of our 'C' roads. Coaches and large vehicles had to drive anti-clockwise round the 'Rings of Kerry'. This involved driving along the mountainside, whereas the other vehicles had a sheer drop of many feet into valleys below. Many wild flowers were growing along the side of the road. One prolific species was montbretia; this was everywhere regardless of soil conditions. There was also wild fuchsia with colourful red 'drops', known as Irish girls' tears. Bracken grew abundantly and local people called it 'fairy duvets'; before duvets came in it was blankets! Heather was in bloom and we saw a donkey with panniers full, and selling to tourists. Some scenery was like Cumbria and even the Brecon Beacons.

The first stop was at 'Bog Village' where a museum showed how turf was harvested from the local bogs for burning on household fires. Several fields had ready-cut turf placed to dry and then carried to the houses.

Entrance to Bog Village museum

When we returned to the coach, we had a rendition of *The Rose of Tralee* from our guide. He explained that the following week there was a ladies' musical festival competition final in Tralee. Every year competitions were held all over Ireland to find a lady with a beautiful voice to be crowned the winner, TV and radio making the winner a celebrity.

Much of the living accommodation consisted of bungalows and these were mostly painted in cream and white, or yellow, although there were no restrictions on colour. The modern homes looked very luxurious from the outside. We were told they cost about £200,000 on the western side of Kerry. Homes were scattered in the countryside and with a good distance apart. The population in southern Ireland was approximately 4.5 million.

The languages, we were told, had a similarity to the Gaelic languages; all had similar spellings although they were pronounced differently. Many fields on the farms were rough compared to the English; ragwort was prolific although it was supposed to be removed as it is poisonous to cattle. We know Ireland has a lot of wet weather; this makes the fields green, hence it is known as the 'Emerald Isle'. The saint of Kerry is St Brendan.

We stopped to view the Dingle Peninsula across the stretch of water, this being open to the Atlantic Ocean with strong gale force winds. The winters were not cold owing to the gulf stream, which helps to maintain the temperature. Sometimes the caps of the mountains have snow. Wind farms had been placed on the sides of the mountains but had to be removed as this caused landslides. We noticed there were several circles of stones that were thought to be Bronze Age; these were mostly in the mountain ranges.

A man from history, Daniel O'Connell, became a wealthy man after studying to become a lawyer in France and smuggling wine into Ireland. There were so many coves it made the smuggling easy. Daniel eventually became a member of parliament in 1828 and was known as the liberator of the penal laws. We also learnt that Valentia Island, at the mouth of an inlet, was where the first overseas cable had been laid for telephones and used until the 1950s.

Our lunch break was near Cahersiveen in a restaurant overlooking the harbour and some islands, such a beautiful view. The restaurant was a special coach stop for meals and while five coaches were parked, we were served almost immediately, the service was so quick, and all home-cooked meals.

View from restaurant

Later a short stop was made where Charlie Chaplin had connections and a statue of him was on the promenade. Sneem was the next place to stop but it was raining again. There was a bridge there which was perfect for a photograph. The stream rushed under the bridge and divided the village. At the national park we stopped for the 'Ladies View', so called as Queen Victoria came here and her entourage looked down to the three lakes in 1846. There was a large island in Lough Leane (from 'Loch Lein', meaning 'lake of learning') which years ago had a monastery.

Ladies View

We continued on to Muckross House. This was situated in a very large park with many oak trees. In the past 9 million trees had been used in ship building and pit props in coal mines. Sheep roamed around in the area; also there were many pine forests in various stages of growth, on the mountains and high hills. Remains of cottages could be seen where they had been deserted in the potato famine around 1840. During this period many people died of malnutrition. There were 9 million people who died and 3 million emigrated, leaving just 3 million behind.

In 1929 Muckross House and the 4000 acres surrounding it were donated to the nation and now the grounds are a national park. The house was restored to its original Victorian state and is now open to the public. The gardens extend to many acres and are a very peaceful place.

Top: Muckross House. Bottom: Ross Castle.

Killarney was the largest town in the area and we toured around it before going to Ross Castle. Unfortunately it was pouring with rain so we did not go far. We did hear a little of its history; in 1649 it was the last place to resist Oliver Cromwell. It was thought no one would storm the castle owing to the lake, but Cromwell crushed the rebels and, knowing the circumstances, entered the last stronghold via the lake and its owner O'Donoghue surrendered.

The town of Killarney had 9000 residents in off peak season and 40,000 when the visitors arrived. St Mary's Cathedral was used as a hospital for sick and orphaned children in the 1840s not long after it had been built.

We noticed that pop music was not heard here! Only Irish music; there was always time to sing their songs. Our guide sang in the coach on the way to the airport. Although most of the time it was raining we had a good day out, interesting and to be recommended. Jenny, my companion, has already booked a return ticket.

Zambia, Botswana and South Africa
October 2004
(three weeks)

This time it was a ten-hour flight from Heathrow to Johannesburg, known locally as Jo'burg. As we left London the pilot explained the aircraft now weighed 380 tons on take-off, and 156 tons was fuel. The speed at lift-off was 227 miles per hour, which increased as we climbed higher, eventually reaching 31,000 feet above ground. The speed increased as the weight of fuel decreased.

In Jo'burg we were met by a guide. The group gathered together not knowing who was going to be on the tour from the flight; this included our English rep who had flown with us. Twenty-four met Karylin who led us for the complete tour. A long walk to our coach and then a wait as our passengers gathered together. While we sat on the coach a young black lad came rushing out of a building followed by a security man chasing him. He had obviously taken something from there; about five minutes later the pair returned with the lad in handcuffs! The coaches had an anti-theft lock fitted to prevent trouble.

The driver took us to our destination, which was Sun City. This was a two-hour journey with a stop on the way for refreshments. Noel, our guide, had been doing the work for the past ten years; he gave an insight into the country by giving a commentary most of the journey. We travelled on the outskirts of the town, on to a motorway, driving the same side of the road as in England. Speed limits were designated up to 120 miles per hour. We passed factories including one of Siemens', not far from a shanty town for workers. There were also many unemployed people sitting by the side of the road hoping someone would stop and offer them work. The present unemployment figure was 44% in that particular area but over the whole of South Africa it was 29%.

Gold was mined, but now up to 4000 feet below ground and only 300 tons mined per year. Owing to the depth of the mine where the people worked it was very hot; cold air and water had to be pumped down to them. Gold was originally discovered by an Australian. Between towns were kilometres of completely deserted areas with no habitation.

Platinum was being mined away from the towns, hence more shanty towns had grown up for the workers. Eighty percent of platinum reserves were being sold for $850 per ounce. This area was only 860 feet above sea level. There were 54 million people living in South Africa; immigrants from bordering countries were arriving every day, and when discovered were returned to their country of origin. This was becoming a lost cause as they returned to South Africa as soon as possible. There were no real borders with barriers hence it was easy to return. Zulu-speaking tribes consisted of 14 million people.

Electricity was made from coal from 17 coal mines, three hydro plants and one nuclear station which provided the national grid. Even some shanty towns had electricity provided the people could afford to pay for it.

Trees had originally been imported from several countries, including Australia and Mexico. There were 2 million hectares of manmade forest. Most of the fir trees were used for pit props in the mines or for paper. It was the time of year for jacarandas to bloom so everywhere there were blue trees, and also many of the seven varieties of bougainvillea were in flower beside the road. Masses of acacia with thorns; animals eat the leaves but do not touch the wood. The rainfall is 25 inches a year in the northern part of South Africa. The soil is very poor here and even maize is difficult to grow. There are some so-called smallholdings which have up to 100 acres.

On our journey we passed the cave where Professor Broom found one of the earliest prehistoric skulls in Sterkfontein not far from the Lesedi Village. A large lake had been dammed to irrigate thousands of hectares. We passed through the

Magaliesberg mountains. One side was dry with a considerable amount of granite and the other side had more fertile soil; orchards of fruit grew here, mostly oranges and pecan nuts, to be exported to Holland. Many of the mountains were extinct volcanoes. A bridge took us over the crocodile river, but no crocodiles; they are only seen in national parks.

There are 55 different types of snakes here and two of the most poisonous and dangerous are the black mamba and the puff adder, they only cause trouble if disturbed and not able to escape. Very few horses were around owing to the sickness which kills them. Ostriches are farmed; a male is black after 18 months of age and the female grey. When their eggs are laid the male takes a turn sitting on them at night.

Sun City, 187 kilometres from Jo'berg, was the first resort where we were to stay and on entering a toll had to be paid. In 1976 the city was established and completely enclosed with all the amenities including casinos and shops. There were timeshare units, a golf course. Our hotel was the Palace hotel and situated within some gardens. This was one of three hotels. We had actually been booked in at one of the others but something was wrong with the swimming pool so we were upgraded. This hotel had been a tribal palace and only the best of everything was in the building. Bird life was prolific and dawn chorus at its best. Transport was provided anywhere within the city and free. We were invited to make the most of it, as we had to remain within the city walls for safety.

The actual palace had been built centuries ago in tribute to the tribe's royal family. It had been rediscovered and the splendour has been restored. It was unbelievable when first entering with the decor and architecture. The entrance was high with several wild animals depicted in metal in different poses; in the entrance hall were paintings on the ceiling of plants and animals.

When going to register we were all given glasses of orange juice. The decorations contained many elephant tusks. Just outside the reception was a life-sized statue of an elephant. Rosemary and I were allocated room 2052, which was very lavishly furnished, with wooden headboards, and then a heavy wooden sliding door revealed a large en suite bathroom with polished marble floors and surround to the wash basins.

Top and bottom: Palace hotel, Sun City

The remainder of the day we were left to recuperate from our flight. One thing we noticed was that all staff spoke and gave a broad smile when met in a corridor.

Breakfast was in the main hall, which had large statues in the centre of the room. There was a large choice of food, Mexican, Japanese and continental. Each time we lifted a drink or food from a tray it was carried for us back to our table. We were literally waited on hand and foot by the waiters and waitresses. The temperature was warm enough for us to sit on the terrace without a cardigan; it was 23°C.

After breakfast our group met outside by 7.45am ready to go and visit Pilanesberg Game Reserve on safari. The vehicle was a long-based Jeep with a canvas roof and no sides other than a safety rail. We were taken a few kilometres down the road and into the park; we were all given a bottle of water as the atmosphere was hot and dry. Once inside the park the driver (and guide) took a gun out of its case and loaded it for safety. We had only just gone inside when a hyena crossed in front of us. Remarks and excitement went through our group; what else would we be seeing? During the drive we saw over 20 different species of animals, including rhino, elephant, zebra, baboon, gnu and antelope.

One of the most memorable moments for me was when a rhino was tranquilised from a helicopter for tagging. We saw it fall and the people rush to its side and do what was necessary, then it was injected to come round, and all the workers rushed to their Land Rover to get out of the way. When an animal comes round from an anaesthetic it can become disorientated and can be very dangerous. The Land Rover moved some distance from the rhino and waited watching for it to come to its feet. The animal then slowly moved away and joined another rhino! This was not purely for tourists but something that is done when required. When the helicopter flew overhead it disturbed a warthog. The animal ran scared with its tail at 90 degrees to its back. It really was amusing to see it run with such a spindly tail like that!

This reserve did not contain any tigers, but had several lions. In a special enclosure two lions had been placed to get used to people and the area as they had been moved from another park, to get fresh blood in the breeding. Already a female outside had taken a fancy to them. She had definitely decided on one of the males. When the lions were in this pen they were fed, but had no contact with anyone.

Top and bottom: Pilanesburg Park, rhino and zebra

Often mixed species of animals lay together as a safety precaution, as an example we saw antelope and wildebeest together. Hippos wallowed in a lake with a white-headed fish eagle on the bank. Weaver birds had made nests in acacia trees; the nests hung down like bottles from the branches in clusters.

The park was formed in 1979 and consists of 150,000 acres. Not unlike the New Forest in England controlled burning of some areas takes place; this encourages new growth for feeding the animals, but it can take four years for the re-growth.

At one point 50 elephants had to be imported from another reserve; the animals were four to six years old but caused so much trouble, including killing several rhinos, that six older elephants had to be brought in to teach the youngsters manners and how to behave.

There are 1800 elephants and 40 lions in the park, amongst other animals. If there are sick animals they become someone's lunch in the wild. I saw a zebra with a swollen foot; the rangers were not allowed to treat it; the guide said it would probably become the lions' next meal. Hippos can run as fast as 35 kilometres an hour, yet they look so clumsy. They are the most dangerous animal in the reserve.

By this time the temperature had risen to 28 or 29°C, and hats were welcome, also a breeze was blowing as we travelled. Later we found several of us had sunburn, including myself when my nose suffered!

The original tribe in the reserve called themselves names of various animals, then would not kill any of those animals, as it would upset the spirits of their ancestors. All tribes had been moved out of the reservation and given an area outside.

This tour took us four hours, this becoming one of the outstanding memories.

The hotel employed many staff at the entrance. I counted ten waiting to help clients into the hotel; they had living quarters in some buildings not far from the hotel. A wedding party was going on during the evening; we got in the lift with the bride and groom. The bride's dress was white and embroidered with gold thread, it really looked beautiful. Some of our time was spent sitting beside the large hotel swimming pool where I watched a bird nesting in one of the palm trees.

Thursday morning we had an early call at 5am as we were to fly to Livingstone in Zambia. To get there we had to go back to Jo'burg. The hotel packed a breakfast to take with us to eat on the way. Our guide gave us more information as we travelled in the coach. Schooling for children had to be paid for by parents, and this cost between 800 and 1800 rand per month (ten rand to the English pound.) People were means tested so the lower paid were able to obtain some help. Even so many children ran the distance to school; this makes sense as many black people in athletics have more stamina then many white on long-distance running; they started young.

Our guide stated that after saving for 40 years towards a pension he will only receive 760 rand per month. Today many people only have two children owing to the cost. Very few cycles were seen on the roads; this was owing to the danger with other vehicles.

After one hour 30 minutes' flight, which included lunch, we arrived at Livingstone airport. What a greeting, 34°C! It really felt hot and we were pleased to walk into a cooler building to register our entry and collect our luggage, which was laid out on a table; there was no conveyer belt. This was just a very small airport, so they had not spent on machinery for passengers. The air-conditioned coach met us with bottles of cold water. We had to be careful not to get dehydrated.

Livingstone was named after the famous explorer David Livingstone in 1905. The Victoria Falls were named after Queen Victoria, but she never had the opportunity to visit them. A rich culture now revolves round the falls, and the Island of Livingstone where David lived for some time.

We were now in Zambia; this was part of Rhodesia in the past. It was suggested that we not go out of the grounds of the hotel on our own. As we were on the borders of the country, there was high unemployment; money was a great attraction to steal from tourists. After a 20-minute drive we saw the hotel Livingstone, where we were allocated our rooms. Rosemary and I had a ground-floor suite facing the gardens and river. It was possible to see the spray from the falls while lying in bed! The river had an electric fence along the perimeter, to prevent wild animals and unwanted immigrants coming in to the garden. The grounds had wild animals such as zebra, giraffes and many monkeys. We could not leave doors or windows open as the monkeys would come in and steal anything and everything. We were told to respect all animals; they were wild and could bite, scratch and kick!

A trip on the Zambezi had been arranged with a barbecue and other refreshments on board. The main idea was to watch the sunset over the river and any animals come down to drink at the edge of the water. The only animals we saw were hippos and one or two crocodiles at the edge. The sunset was gorgeous with the reflection in the water. The boat was called the *African Queen*; it was said it was the original but I very much doubt it! This was such a pleasant journey.

Next morning was so warm we had breakfast on the terrace. No coats or cardigans were required while on this tour. There was a good selection of fruit juices such as orange, guava, kiwi, or a cocktail of them plus more. We were then invited to a cooked or continental breakfast.

Before the temperature rose too high a guide took us on a two-hour walk to see the actual falls. Karylin the guide said she was disappointed as she was there in April and the falls were in full spate, whereas there was now only a small amount falling into the river below. The walk ended at a local market, selling things the people had made. By this time the temperature had risen even more. The coach driver went to fetch the coach to take us to the hotel. When he arrived the fan belt broke, so we ended up by walking to the hotel.

Some information about the Victoria Falls: the river Zambezi is 2900 kilometres long. When in full spate 550 gallons of water fall every second. There are five sections to the Falls and a 90-foot drop from top to bottom where it falls into a dead volcano. There were many dragonflies of several colours. White water rafting could be seen close to the bridge which separates Zambia from Zimbabwe; at this time it was a 'no go' area for tourists. The two countries are not very friendly so we were strictly forbidden to go near the bridge. Some of our group saw the Falls from the air, but Rosemary and I found it would be too expensive by air.

Top: Victoria Falls. Bottom: bridge separating Zambia and Zimbabwe.

By the time we returned to the hotel, the monkeys were everywhere in the grounds; many were carrying their babies. The young always faced the way they were travelling; mum's teat was handy to hang on to, and tails wrapped round mother's tail. We spent some time watching their antics, which caused much laughter. One group could be called teenagers; they had marvellous fun playing. In the evening we used one of the golf buggies to get round the grounds and to the restaurant for the evening meal. Although we were many miles from the sea, fish and chips were served.

The highlight for me was the trip to Botswana. It was an hour's journey in the coach; most of the road was more like Australia, as it was possible to see miles ahead. We passed many villages of mud huts and children walking to school, some young ones carrying water in plastic containers on their heads, as there was little or no water available in the village. Much of the scenery was scorched bushes and trees along the side of the road, waiting for rains due in about three weeks' time.

Eventually we came to the border between Zambia and Botswana; it was not what we expected. Many lorries at the border contained equipment for food; cars were beside the road being searched. The police control had a decent building, but the remainder of the buildings were just shacks! The only way to cross to Botswana was across the river; the large vehicles and cars crossed on a ferry, but pedestrians crossed in a small motor boat which seated ten people. There was no real pier to get into these small boats on either side of the river bank. A coach was waiting for us on the other side, and took us to the Lodge hotel; from there we boarded a larger boat, for coffee and biscuits before pulling away from the pier.

The cruise took us to a larger river to see all the wild animals that came down to graze or drink from the water, and came close to us on an island. In a rainy season the island is completely covered up to three metres with water where the river has burst its banks. When the water was shallow the animals just walked across the river to the islands. While we were in the middle of the river we were on the boundaries of four countries, namely Zambia, Zimbabwe, Botswana and Namibia, and also in the Chobe National Park.

Top: getting on the boat. Bottom: Chobe reserve.

There were many species of animals, including 6000 elephants; 400 of these live beside the river, drinking or wallowing in mud. While we watched one of the babies wandered off from the family group. It was not long before the matriarch realised the circumstances and so chased after it, trumpeting loudly. Baby squealed and rushed back into the group while being followed by a gentle push. We were amused and thought even animals correct their young, when humans are not allowed to by law; who is right? A fully grown bull elephant can weigh six tons and a female five and a half tons; a newborn baby weighs 120 kilos. An elephant can drink as much as 160 litres of water at one time. The species destroys many trees by rubbing against them to clean their skin.

Three hippos rose out of the water close by; they can weigh up to two tons each and have a skin which can actually become sunburnt! They can also remain under water for up to three minutes. A group (a pod) of hippos contains one male and up to five female in a family. A pregnant female can tell the sex of a baby developing, and if it is a female the mother has the baby within the group; if male she goes away on her own to have the baby and looks after it until it is able to look after itself, then she returns to the pod. The male of the group will kill any other males including a baby.

There were groups of velvet monkeys, many fish eagles, roller birds, which are very colourful, and more than one species of stork. One bird is known as 'Jesus bird' as it walks on the water. There were egrets, pied kingfishers, Egyptian geese, cormorants, plovers, water dippers, almost too many to name. Crocodiles lay on the river banks; they can last for two months without eating, and are very protective towards their young as they hatch. Antelope, waterbuck, warthogs and impalas were scattered along the banks and on the islands. Warthogs give birth to young in September and October. Waterbuck have a gland which makes their coat waterproof; when they are scared they dive for the water. Giraffes are browsers and when the park is dry they disappear into more sheltered areas amongst the trees. It is not necessary for them to drink water, due to the moisture in the leaves they eat, and they can live to the age of 35 years.

Top: crocodile on the bank. Bottom: hippos and elephants.

Regarding the impalas, it is possible for them to synchronise their young births according to the weather. They wait for the rains to come so there is sufficient grass for them to graze and produce milk for the babies. Small jellyfish are in the river; we also saw a water snake.

After the full morning gliding around in the boat, to and fro to see any birds or animals close to the bank, we returned to the pier; new steps had been fixed to the boat, and there was movement in the water. I went to put my foot on the pier and fell over; luckily the camera was not damaged, only a biro doubled in half!

A buffet lunch was served in the Lodge hotel, and was really enjoyed by everyone. Afterwards two safari Jeeps took our group into the bush in the park. Most of the ground was very sandy and our Jeep had a shovel, on the vehicle itself, and a container with bottles of water for guests. We saw kudus, which had horns that twisted; each twist represented a year of the animals' lives. As they got older so the horns became longer, and on the underside of the neck and brisket the hair grew longer. Large nests of approximately three feet square had little birds nesting in the base, while large birds sat on the top.

Unfortunately anthrax was prevalent in buffalos and there had been 500 deaths, hence all vehicles' wheels, and guests' shoes, had to be disinfected before and after entry into the reserve.

One tree had fruit which looked like sausages hanging from the branches; the tribes made use of these as medicine. They scraped out the contents of the fruit then soaked them in water and gave that water to the children for colds or stomach problems, sometimes bathing them in the liquid. Balsa wood was also used for upset stomachs. By the time we had driven right into the bush it was the hottest part of the day and many animals sheltered out of the sun; this made it more difficult to see them. As the day finished more people came into the park; they would have better views of the animals.

After this enjoyable outing we returned by coach to the borders for the river crossing back to Zambia. We hit some large waves and some of us got very wet. This was a day I will never forget, it was such an enjoyable outing. While I was on this trip Rosemary went on a short one not far from our hotel.

Sunday morning we had breakfast on the terrace; the temperature had risen by the time we had finished. Monkeys were once again up to mischief. Security chased them off our grounds with sticks and catapults, only to turn round and walk back followed by the monkeys! This morning we were taken by motor boat across to Livingstone Island where we were greeted with glasses of mango juice by a waiter; this was delicious. We walked to a different area to get a view of Victoria Falls, with a double rainbow over them. After the walk we were treated to coffee and cakes under the shade of a gazebo. Two people remain on the island the whole time to look after nature's fauna and flora. Elephants had been on the island as we were shown their footprints, and hippos were heard honking in the river.

This day was the fortieth anniversary of Independence Day for Zambia, but as a bank holiday it was saved until the Monday. Back at the hotel grounds and lawns were being sprayed to deter the malaria mosquitoes; this made sitting by the pool more comfortable. Being on our last day in this area we made the most of the garden and river scenes before returning to the airport. There were two flights leaving, one being ours. Many people were there, but there was no air conditioning in the building, so it was extremely hot.

We arrived at Cape Town two hours later; it was dark by the time we reached our hotel, 'The Table Bay'. Our windows overlooked the harbour and Table Mountain. The mountain was lit up for the evening. We had an early night after the travelling.

We saw the top of Table Mountain when we got up next morning; there were no clouds or mist. The mist that often hangs over the mountain is called a table cloth. This often denotes high winds making it too dangerous for visitors to remain on the top. We enjoyed breakfast on the terrace surrounded by seagulls. A gentleman brought his breakfast and put it on a table, then realised he had left the cutlery inside. He went back in to collect it, and a gull came down and took his sausage off his plate and flew off with it. You could not trust any birds; they would snatch any food!

Later we went up Table Mountain as it was still clear; we took the cable car up which took 65 people at one time. The car travels at a maximum of ten metres per second and each car weighs 18 tons. If there is a wind, water ballast is added for safety, up to 4000 litres at one time. The views were great from this height going up to the top.

Top: cable car. Bottom: the tablecloth over Table Mountain.

Table Mountain at the highest point is 1085 metres. This region is renowned for the flora and fauna as there are over 1500 species. There are concerns on how to protect several species including protea, as well as wildlife and birds. Red-winged starlings are quite common. A hyrax resembles a rabbit and is native to the mountain. It is not a rodent, but its closest relation is an elephant.

Half an hour after our arrival on the top of the mountain the klaxon sounded for us to return to the bottom as the table cloth was going to cover the top. When we arrived at the bottom the mountain was already covered with mist.

A coach had arrived to take us on a tour of Cape Town. Early settlers were of Dutch origin and street names still remain in Afrikaans, a language rooted in Dutch. It was not until 1811 that some English people arrived bringing English names. On the Royal Observatory a cannon is fired at midday except on Sundays.

On tour outside Cape Town

August is the coldest time of the year, when snow can sometimes be seen on the highest points of mountains around the area.

February is the hottest month. Robben Island, where Mandela was imprisoned for many years, is not far out to sea; before becoming a prison it was a hospital for leprosy. In 1994 apartheid was stopped and people of all races were allowed to mix.

Adjoining the hotel was a large shopping complex that consisted of three floors and over 100 shops, which we visited. Rosemary took a helicopter trip round the Cape, where she saw some whales. In the evening she went out on a sailing boat. When she returned in the dark at 8pm she spoke of the choppy sea and large waves which soaked everyone on board; everyone enjoyed the experience and had a good laugh!

The following morning was cooler so we had breakfast inside; no seagulls appeared outside! The coach collected us for another tour, this time to Kirstenboch National Garden. This was called a living museum with wild and protected plants. The gardens are actively involved in research and environmental education. Kirstenboch is situated on the eastern slopes of Table Mountain with over 528 hectares. A special Braille Trail and fragrance garden had been planted and guided tours could be obtained. I must mention the special protea borders; as this is the national flower of South Africa, there are many species of this planted in separate areas.

Even in prehistoric times people lived in the area; it was surveyed by Jan van Riebeeck in 1652 and stone axes were found. In 1660 a group of shipwrecked French refugees on the way to Madagascar were employed to plant a wild almond hedge. Cecil John Rhodes bought ground in 1895 for £9000 and this was left to the nation in 1902 when Rhodes died; part of this land became Kirstenboch. I would have loved to have spent longer walking round the gardens.

When being driven towards the cape we passed through Constantia where the most expensive houses had been built, one resident being the former prime minister Margaret Thatcher's son. The Australian oaks were in bloom with yellow flowers. It was mentioned that 11 languages were spoken in South Africa. We travelled southwest. The guide gave more information regarding the area which had become a national reserve; wild animals were allowed to roam freely but not all were visible, but there were ostriches, baboons and various antelope, not forgetting all the wild flowers. They flowered at different times during the year, so there was always something in bloom. At the actual cape, several people went up to see the lighthouse. I sat outside a restaurant and watched some lizards on a wall, then whales came into the bay and surfaced for air; there were six; they come to the bay to have their calves.

The road was very narrow on our way to Simon's Town, where we had lunch. For many years the port was occupied by the English navy, but they had pulled out a few years before. The railway to Cape Town and further north ran along the edge of the cliffs; sometimes it had to be closed owing to rough seas.

A colony of penguins near the Cape of Good Hope

The afternoon took us to a colony of penguins in False Bay where they were wild but tolerated visitors standing and watching them. Several were in the process of moulting; this takes 14 days. The colony are African and because they bray like a donkey they are called 'jackass penguins'. They swim at an average speed of seven kilometres an hour. Their enemies are sharks and cape fur seals, mongooses, gannets, cats and dogs; gulls will steal an opportunity if it arises. The main breeding season is during February and there are approximately a thousand penguins living in this area. A South African society that looks after sea birds called SANCCOB treated 2000 sick birds during 2003. Many of the problems were caused by pollution along the coast.

The last day of the holiday arrived and this was spent in the wine region as South African wine is well known in England. There were many acres of vineyards, some owned privately and others by a large Co-operative. One of the centres made red and white wine. For the red they use the skins added to the juice; this gives extra flavour. In some vineyards roses were planted at the ends of the rows; they show disease as soon as it appears in the vines. The town of Paarl is very Dutch and many slaves were brought here during the past to work. Many houses here were thatched with reeds, and the earliest house built in 1749.

We went on to Stellenbosch which is the oldest town in the area outside Cape Town, founded in 1679, and started with some French immigrants. There is now a large university with 1600 attending. They helped to build the original fruit farms and vineyards. The soil is very fertile so pears, apples, peaches and oranges are grown there, plus wheat and protea; there is also share farming.

After all this it was time to make our way home via Cape Town airport and back to the UK after 11 hours' flying.

What did I think of this holiday? Fantastic! We both enjoyed the holiday so much, a pleasant atmosphere with fellow travellers, the hotels first-class, Karylin the leader was very helpful and everything went smoothly. A holiday to remember.

Paris
June 2005
(weekend visit)

This time a weekend away in Paris, and yes it was special with my partner Clive (who I have since married). We decided at short notice to make the visit. It was only 45 minutes' flying time from Bournemouth airport to Charles de Gaulle just north of Paris. A bus was taken to Montparnasse, and from there we travelled by taxi to our hotel; the journey cost 15 euros. There was an enormous amount of traffic travelling on all roads. Most of the cars were small, only one or two four-by-fours and nothing bigger.

The reception at the hotel was very basic, rooms were clean and comfortable and breakfast in the morning. After unpacking we went for a walk around the area and found a restaurant for an evening meal. It was here we met a man called Guy, who was French but spoke good English. Eventually we found out he represented France at EU meetings. On his recommendation we had a steak to eat. It was noticed on the way back to the hotel that vehicles just parked when and where they liked, even on a zebra crossing. Pavements were very rough in places, no signs to warn of the state of the pavement.

The following day at breakfast we met a Canadian couple from Toronto. After studying the map we went by metro to the opera house. This was a large building which had gilt on the outside; it was also a famous place to make arrangements to meet people. The main tourist buses parked behind the building, the 'hop on, hop off' open top. Our first stop was at Notre Dame Cathedral, but before going in we had a coffee at one of the pavement cafés. The cathedral is somewhere I will always remember; we sat quietly in one of the chapels before lighting two candles. It was fascinating with large stained-glass windows, wooden carvings and monuments, one for Joan of Arc. Although many people were visiting in the cathedral it was very quiet and peaceful. We did not go into the tower as there were queues waiting to go up. Lunch was sandwiches we had brought, and we sat on a wall outside.

After this we walked to find our way round; this included several miles through public gardens where aerobics were taking place. A group of young people were demonstrating at quite a pace. From here we walked on to the Place de la Concorde and then on to the river Seine to the École Militaire. We passed many expensive floating restaurants; one boat was able to cater for 1000 people. After all this we walked to a café for an evening meal before returning to the hotel by metro. Some time was spent resting our weary feet; little was thought about after returning to the hotel but a good night's sleep.

Most shops closed on a Sunday and there were only one or two places where a meal could be obtained. We were late for breakfast having tired ourselves out the previous day. Again we took the metro and hopped onto the tourist bus. After seeing the Champs-Élysées and the Arc de Triomphe for the second day, we alighted at the Eiffel Tower.

The queues were long to go to the top; it was not worth waiting so we went on one of the Bateaux Parisiens for a trip down the Seine. On the cruise it was possible to see more of Paris including the Bastille. It was peaceful gliding down the river, under 20 of the 36 bridges including the 'Kissing Bridge'. A small island in the centre of the river was where Paris originated, and contained many old buildings. Photographs had been taken when we had boarded the boat, and we bought one on returning to the quay. After this we returned to the hotel.

It was time to return to England; most of the day was spent waiting around, then another 45-minute flight back to Bournemouth airport. A happy weekend, 'up and away'.

Top: Champs-Élysées. Bottom: house boats on the Seine

Isle of Man
July 2005
(day trip)

One more day trip from Hurn airport with only three quarters of an hour in the air, so no breakfast, just a cup of coffee. As expected just a small airport with the Manx flag flying. We took an anticlockwise tour of the island. It is only three miles long and 16 miles wide. Originally the Duke of Athol owned the island but he gave the island to England. The islanders consider themselves to be independent with 23 members on their Tynwald parliament and this has been so for 1000 years.

Not long after leaving the airport we saw large herds of Charolais cattle grazing in the very green fields. In the past I visualised moors and hills, but I was pleasantly surprised to see beautiful countryside, with woods and streams, gorges and undulating land with crops of corn. There were several breeds of beef cattle. The dairy herds were mostly in the northern area. Roads were mostly narrow except in the urban areas.

The Thomas the Tank Engine film *Thomas and the Magic Railroad* was shot near the town of Douglas, also some other well-known films were made in the same places. Some of the house owners lived in the back of the house while films were being made at the front. Manx people are very superstitious, and the Fairy Bridge has to be greeted when passing over it. It is important to be polite and to say hello to 'themselves'; if you forget you may have to pay a price!

Douglas contains a third of the population for the whole island, and is also the capital. At a glance it looked like Weymouth with many Victorian houses along a two-mile promenade. Most of the shops were small, some with well-known names such as the Body Shop and Marks and Spencer; the shopping precinct ran parallel to the promenade. The goods were expensive as they had to be imported from England. Horse-drawn trams were used in the town; these had been used since 1876, and were the oldest working trams in the world. At the time of the visit petrol was 91 or 92 pence per litre, ten pence more than at home. The currency used was mostly English but they also had their own. The people were very friendly and we were welcomed. There were only two breweries left on the island.

As we continued our tour the driver, who also acted as our guide, told us on January 8 2005 450 trees were blown down in a storm and they blocked many roads. On the island there are either gale force winds or no wind at all, no happy medium! They have very few frosts and sometimes a little snow on the tops of the high hills.

Laxey mill

Laxey, which was still further north, was a beautiful little village with tiny roads, only just sufficient room for a coach to crawl through; at one stage there was only about one inch either side of us. This was a former mining village and had a so-called 'New Road' which was built in 1860! There was one special landmark here and that was the 'Laxey Wheel', one of the remnants of the mining era, and still in working condition although the mines were closed in the early 1900s. The miners went to South Africa to work in the later years. Now some of the houses have been given African names. Gardens are now laid out on an area that was in the past used as a washing floor, cleaning and sorting out what had been mined such as lead, zinc and silver.

Snaefell mountain railway

Laxey is the gateway to the highest point of Snaefell which is 2036 feet high; it has an electric railway to the top for tourists. There are 25 other peaks that are at least 1000 feet high on the Isle of Man. There are no snakes, foxes or badgers and consequently there are many ground-nesting birds. In the north there are several hundred feral goats. At the beginning of the

1939–45 war a goat farmer turned all his stock into the wild, as he had to join up in the war. The debate now is over how they can be controlled. Flocks of sheep were all round the island. One famous breed native to the island is called Loaghtan; they mostly have four horns. The meat is expensive and is sold in restaurants.

We stopped at Ramsey, which means 'wild garlic'; this was once a ship-building town. Victorian buildings were popular. One door was built extra high; this was for a man who stood seven feet, ten inches tall! He went to France with a circus and supposedly died, but a few years later he was seen in New York; this was an insurance scam.

Many houses were built with the local quarry stone and several had a pebbledash finish. We were driven on to visit Peel, which was on the river, and a large castle on the hill. Port Erin, another town, was on the south coast; it was here we all enjoyed a barbecue on the promenade, and timed things just right, as it started to rain as we reached the coach. We travelled through Castletown and finally back to the airport, and home.

What were my thought on the Isle of Man? Beautiful countryside; very few places of interest to visit, but grand for people who wish to go for a walking holiday.

Salzburg and the Lakes
August 2005
(day trip)

Just a day trip but we had to report at the airport at 6am. It took one and a half hours' flying time, instead of two hours; we had a tail wind, and travelled at 600 miles an hour.

Horst was the Austrian guide. Salzburg was a very small place 2500 years ago, historians had been able to trace back. In the sixteenth century a third of the world's gold, zinc and salt had been mined in this region, hence the name Salzburg, meaning 'salt city'. The river was the main way of transporting materials in boats from the mountains. There are 70 lakes in close proximity all surrounded by mountains. The origin of people living here goes back to Italy and Germany. One mountain has a television station and is 1806 metres high (nearly 6000 feet!).

Since 1945 the population has doubled. Two thousand students arrive each year to study the music of Mozart, as he lived in the town. We visited St Gilgen on the Wolfgang Lake. The village has very narrow streets and a house where Mozart's mother was born. The houses are typical design for Austria, often with large paintings on the outside walls.

Wolfgang Lake is 150 metres deep. A hotel was placed on the pinnacle of a mountain nearby, 1800 metres above sea level. It can be seen from the lake and is used all the year round. The villages round the lake are 175 metres above sea level.

Most of the group that day took a scenic cruise across the lake to St Wolfgang; the remainder, us included, went by coach. We too had a beautiful scenic drive, to meet the others. The village had been named after a bishop from the fourteenth century. Most churches were of the Catholic faith with some very elaborate decorations. Some mountains were 2900 metres high, and were of limestone; this showed between the pine or beech trees on the side of the mountain. Lake Hallstatt is eight kilometres long and 56 metres deep; the name means 'holy salt'. This place is some distance from Salzburg and until 1989 a passport was required to enter this area.

St Wolfgang

The scenery was beautiful with many of us saying we wished to return there. The village nestles into the side of the mountain with a waterfall. Houses had been built high above one another into the side of the mountain. A funicular was available to take people to the top where some salt mines remained. Years ago miners worked in the mines for four days at the time and the women carried the salt down to the base.

There was limited space for the burial of the dead, as the ground was mostly hard rock; we were told 20 years after they had been buried, they were then dug up and their bones placed in the 'Bone House' so the graves could be re-used. We did not see this house but it sounded very gruesome! In the past the Hapsburg family owned the lake; it was used for hunting and fishing, particularly wild boar and deer. Many large lodges had been built around the perimeter of the lake.

A view of the lake.

After having to leave this beautiful place we travelled on to Attersee, before passing on to Mondsee for another break. The church here had been used in the filming of *The Sound of Music*, as it was very old and picturesque.

After this we had to return to the airport and home. Many people said it was the best tour they had ever been on; I was very much in agreement and hope to return there one day, it was so beautiful.

Top: the village of St Wolfgang. Bottom: the village church.

Dublin, Ireland
October 2005
(four days)

Clive and I flew from Hurn to Dublin airport in 55 minutes, taking one of the airport buses to O'Connell Street. It was here we saw the millennium monument: a pole pointed like a needle, and known locally as 'The Stiletto in the Ghetto'. This cost £3 million and stands 136 metres high. By this time it was raining so we hailed a taxi to the Harding hotel in Fishamble Street; this was in the older part of the town. After booking in we went for a walk around the area.

Opposite the hotel was Christ Church Cathedral; adjoining it was a museum showing Dublin through the ages. We thought the exhibition had been very carefully planned and made interesting for children as it was 'hands on'. There were brass rubbings, and smelling different spices which had been imported. Our tour through the building took nearly an hour, with the contents covering Dublin from 1170 to 1540. The display was owned by the Medieval Trust and had no financial help from the government.

From this building we entered the cathedral for the Church of Ireland, which is also part of the Anglican Communion. It is the mother church of Dublin and Glendalough. A Viking cathedral was originally built on this site in 1030 and Laurence O'Toole was its first archbishop. Major restorations have taken place over the centuries, the latest being in 1980–82. There was an enormous crypt which had been used as a marketplace in the early days and was now used for wedding receptions. Preparations were taking place for that evening. The rest of the evening was spent walking

237

miles round the streets, looking in shop windows and eventually returning to the hotel.

The weather forecast for the following day was rain, so we booked a coach tour with Wild Wicklow Tours. Once again the driver also acted as guide. He gave us interesting information as we travelled. First we went through part of Dublin and saw trams carrying people into the city from the suburbs. The river Liffey ran through the centre of Dublin and was tidal, very easy to see. Many older buildings had windows blocked as the result of the glass tax in earlier days. The first member of parliament was a Mr O'Connell and hence the main shopping street was named after him.

The tour took us south to Dun Laoghaire; Holyhead was 56 miles east, and ships travelled to and fro with various goods. During the Napoleonic times the Irish were afraid of the French invading the country, so 56 Martello towers were built along the east coast. These towers had wall three feet thick.

House prices were mentioned as some had been seen up for sale; with three bedrooms a house could cost 345,000 euros, and a one-bedroom flat could cost 270,000 euros. In the Wicklow area, 60% of all farms were sheep, 10% beef and 5% arable. Forestry takes up 10% of the ground, with most of the trees being pine; much of the wood is exported.

Ireland very rarely has snow on the east coast, and in the summer in 2003 the temperature remained between 29 and 32°C for four and a half months.

We followed on down to Dalkey and Killiney, where more prosperous people lived. An interesting stop at Glendalough and a sixth-century monastic settlement: here were the remains of a house with an arch to the doorway made of stone, and this was still standing after all these centuries. We walked through a cemetery that was so old, headstones were standing at all angles, surrounded by long grass. It had not been looked after and some graves were as late as 1960. There was now only sufficient room for five more burials, and the plots had already been booked. There were no inscriptions on the headstones before 1750 as most people were unable to write.

The monastery dated back to 856 when land was plundered by the Vikings. During that time the local people fled to the woods and mountains for safety. The houses in the villages were plundered before being set on fire. When Vikings were on the way monks climbed the tower (approximately 300 feet high) in the cemetery. They climbed an internal staircase to the top window and hung a pole out of the window with burning material to warn people in the valley and nearby high points, and the messages were passed on. After the Vikings left all the houses had to be rebuilt. In 1014 the Vikings were banished from Ireland.

The 'Priest House' which was also known as the 'Whispering House' was where after death monks were laid before burial while prayers were said over the bodies. Only 12 monks lived in this commune at one time and they looked after seven churches.

After all this information we were sent on a walk beside two lakes, through woodland on the side of the mountain where people had once escaped the Vikings. The three quarters of an hour gave us time to look at the local flora and fauna, including ferns and mosses of different types, and to admire the pine and oak trees. The second lake was interesting but the first of more interest with mirror views on the water. This lake was 125 metres deep; everything was very quiet and peaceful.

Houses in the country appeared very isolated and sparse, but there was a pub in the village where we had a home-cooked lunch. After this we continued on our walk. In the mountains it was very misty and this blotted out the many views. A film company were busy taking shots for scenes in a film; many TV programmes are filmed in this area.

Turf had been cut from the mountain bogs and left the countryside scarred. Not many people now use turf for heating their homes. In the past 20 tons would keep an individual home warm for the winter months. After it is first cut it takes 12 weeks to dry sufficiently before being used on fires. The council used to distribute the turf in Dublin for those living there.

One lake we passed was called the 'Guinness Lake' although the correct name was Lough Tay. The reason for the change was that a daughter of the famous family drowned in the lake. There is a memorial beside the lake. The mountains around the lake are 1000 metres high, with sheer drops into the lake. The next stop was at 'Sally's Gap'; the road had been made by the military in the nineteenth century and originally made of oak planks which are now covered with tarmac. The soldiers were stationed in Dublin and were taken out to make the roads. All this was now a national park.

Lough Tay

A shipwreck occurred off the eastern coast and all Germans on board were lost during the Second World War. Some German aircraft crashed into the side of the mountains. The men are now buried near the old garrison. After the war the Germans asked for the bodies to be returned to their homeland. The local council decided that they should remain undisturbed in their graves and gave the piece of land where 136 lay to Germany. The Germans now look after the site where relatives can come and visit. The old garrison is now used for visitors; up to 212 people stay there at one time. People from all countries come to live together to obtain a better understanding of one another. When we stopped in Enniskerry, we looked round the small village; on our return the driver had provided a tot of whisky for everyone!

At the time of our visit road tax on cars and cost for insurance for one driver was over £400, and for a young driver as much as

£7000 depending on the vehicle. Petrol costs were comparable to the English. All cars have to be imported into Ireland, as none are made there.

We returned to Dublin and were given more information on museums and shops as we arrived back. For the evening we walked to the Arlington hotel, where we enjoyed a meal which was followed by an 'Irish' evening of song and dance. They sang some well-known Irish songs for our entertainment.

We took a taxi the following day to the Guinness distillery where we spent a long time looking round, finding our own way as everywhere was marked with the direction we should follow. The Guinness business was started by Arthur Guinness; he bought a 9000-year lease for £100. He had 21 children, hence the large family we hear about. The distillery now consists of 43 acres. The drink is made only of barley and hops. A film was shown with coopers making the barrels; the main man was a Mr Flanagan. Now there are only a few barrels made compared with years ago. Over 50 people were working on the site.

On the seventh floor was a bar and free drink provided; while one drank, a full panoramic view of Dublin could be seen as glass windows were the whole way round the room. It was possible to see for miles especially as the day was clear and sunny.

On leaving the distillery we joined the 'hop on, hop off' bus; there were 20 stops round the city. We decided to dismount first at Kilmainham Jail, which was no longer used as a jail, as it was closed in 1924. It was first used in the eighteenth century, when people were jailed for just small misdemeanours and conditions inside were horrendous. There was one person to a cell but no beds or amenities were provided, only a small hole in the wall where food was pushed through. Many people were hanged in the yard just outside the entrance where local people came to witness the event. Later prisoners were hanged within the prison walls, and even later shot there. When mothers were put inside there was often no one to look after the children so they too came in, sleeping on straw in the corridors outside the cells. At one stage there were as many as five people to a cell and the whole prison had 9000 inmates, when the place was built to manage 170 people. The busiest time was during the uprising in the early 1900s. Éamon de Valera was placed inside at the beginning of the trouble and again when he was president of Southern Ireland in the 1920s.

Inside of the old Kilmainham Jail

We were shown the new wing which is now used for exhibitions. After 1924 when the prison was closed the place was left to deteriorate and trees grew up in the centre of the buildings. A group of ex-prisoners got together and raised sufficient money to restore the buildings and make the old part of the jail a museum.

The 'hop on, hop off' bus took us on to Phoenix Park which included Dublin Zoo. We remained on the bus as the park consisted of over 1000 acres. Many walks and trees were marked with seats to just rest. Football, rugby and cricket pitches were spread through the park. We finally got off at Smithfield, a small village, which is near the city centre. We stopped for refreshments and then went to the Jameson distillery. This was not as large as the Guinness property. They took us on a visitors' tour, although the main part is now in Cork.

We now walked on to O'Connell Street to have the last look at the shops before returning to the hotel. Later we found the Brazen Head, the oldest pub in the city, and had a meal here and then listened to a group of folk singers, with traditional Irish songs.

Alas next morning it was an early trip back to the airport by taxi and the flight home.

The comments on this tour: interesting but another day or two to visit museums would be sufficient before travelling further into the countryside, but then Clive and I are country people!

Fiji
February 2006
(twelve days)

Clive and I reached Fiji two hours 50 minutes after departing Auckland, leaving our daughter Caroline behind to become a resident. This was to have been a four-day stay on the way home. We landed at Nadi airport, which is on the western side of the mainland; a car and guide were waiting for us, as a guided tour on the way to the hotel had been organised earlier. The guide presented us each with a shell garland. The hotel was on an island, which was joined to the mainland by a bridge. We learnt many hotels were situated on the island. Years ago it had been a mango swamp, but this had since been cleared by an Australian firm and some local people. Each hotel had its own private beach.

Our hotel was called Sofitel and was a very luxurious five-star place. Several swimming pools were within the grounds, which we thought was unusual with our own beach. Then we found that the sea was not the best place to swim, with rubbish of all descriptions both floating and lying on the sand. There were many restaurants, both inside and out of the buildings. We ate in the Lagoon Restaurant; this was named after a lagoon in the grounds, but this encouraged the mosquitoes during the evening meals! A buffet was served every evening, with a different menu and a very large selection of food. One ate as much as one wanted. After the meal we walked through the gardens with the gentle and incessant sound of the secondas, small lizards, interspersed with the calming murmur of the waves lapping the lonely beach.

The temperature was between 33 and 34°C with humidity of over 90%. We kept our room at 18°C with air conditioning and every time we went back into the room it really felt cold! Many times we sat down with perspiration running down our faces, and consequently our intake of liquid was quite large! It was strange being surrounded by fruit, both in the trees and at the local market. Juices were much more expensive than beer which contains more water.

The balcony overlooked the beach, with swaying coconut trees, where water and jet skiing could often be seen. On arrival we were given a map to find our way round the hotel as there were so many bedrooms, shops and conference rooms.

Hotel bus

Thatched buses that did not contain any glass in the windows made a circuitous route to all the five hotels every 15 minutes. We found there were three different routes with each having a different colour. We went to the Sheraton hotel to see how it compared with the one where we were staying. We caught a bus – which was free of charge! – to return to our hotel, or so we thought. After doing the circuit three times we realised we were on the wrong bus, so decided to walk after all; it only took ten minutes!

As we walked back on the balmy afternoon we felt strangely insular due to the fact that the causeway to the hotels was monitored by security cameras. Other than the staff we did not encounter any local people from Nadi.

Whenever we returned to the foyer, there was a greeting of 'Bula' (hello) from the friendly staff. We noticed that everywhere we went we were greeted with 'bula'; it did not matter if they were cleaners, garden staff, they were all very polite.

We had arrived in the five-month wet season, so we had a thunderstorm with lightning every afternoon, and the rain poured down for the remainder of the day. Apparently the week before we arrived they had torrential rain, even in the mountains, and water from there flooded Nadi town.

On the Monday morning we did not rise very early. When we had breakfast we were given a glass of champagne!

Like other hotels there was an agent to book the tours. We booked three outings, one day trip and two half-days. The first was a half-day in the afternoon, when a drive was arranged to take us up into the mountains and to a village where the past president had stayed in a thatched cottage. I say 'had stayed' as back in December he and parliamentary members had been turned out of the country in a coup, so now the army ruled the country. Before we left for Fiji it was in the papers that 22 heads of the army had been arrested for embezzling money; that was why the original parliament had been ousted.

There was a Methodist church named after John Wesley, but it had a Fijian spelling. A Bible was handed from John Wesley to a president and is still treasured. We went inside the church, where it was explained that men sat one side and the women and children on the other. They were not allowed to sit together as a family. We were told that only .04% of the population failed to attend church services of one denomination or another. There was a very strong influence of Methodism; Catholics and Hindus were also prevalent. Many services were two hours long. As a consequence of all this, businesses and shops were closed on a Sunday. I remember seeing a Catholic church with people standing outside, as the church was full!

The local people in this village we visited laid out tables with souvenirs and gifts for visitors to purchase, this being one of the area's main incomes.

While on the tour we visited a botanical garden, which had been given to Fiji by Raymond Burr, the actor. There were many different shrubs and trees, and also an amazing 2000 species of orchids. The woman warden knew all the Latin names for them, including the ginger plant: the leaves when rubbed smelt of ginger, also the flowers were very beautiful and colourful. The tour of the garden ended with a punch of fruit juices that was very refreshing and much needed with the high temperature and humidity!

There are many immigrants in the country with the early people originating from India. They helped with the sugar plantations as well as gold mining. When the government released them from slavery, many decided to remain in the country. All the immigrants have the chance to leasehold houses and plots of ground for six months at a time; this can then be renewed. They grow their own vegetables, tapioca and sugar cane and often have a house cow, plus one or two other animals to till the land; these animals pull an old-fashioned one-furrow plough. Families are often large with six to nine children.

While we were travelling in the car a wild mongoose ran in front of us. They are bushy-tailed and a grey-brown colour, the size of a large rat. These were originally imported from India to eat the snakes, and now nearly all the snakes have gone, so now their diet mostly consists of chicken which they take from local people's gardens.

The following day a car safari into the highlands was the tour, travelling miles on unmade roads; some were in a bad state of repair owing to the recent floods, but the scenery was well worth coming to see. There were only one or two scattered houses, and the occasional cluster in a village; our guide lived in a village we had passed. The further we went up into the mountain, the more primitive the houses appeared.

In one village an invitation was given for us to meet people, but we had to adhere to certain rituals, such as wearing a sarong that was provided. The meeting house was in the centre of the village; there everyone sat on the floor and words of welcome were spoken in the local language. The guide explained the way kava would be served and we would be expected to drink some. This was from a root of a tree and dried in the sun, then pummelled into a powder. It was then mixed with water in a ceremonial bowl. A small quantity was given to guests and then to the villagers. This drink if taken in quantity could make the tongue numb and could cause sleep, but was not supposed to be a drug!

One of the women guided us round the village and answered many questions we posed. A stream nearby supplied the water for bathing and washing, also collected for cooking in the home. The houses had little or no furniture, and often more than one family lived together. While walking round we met the chief, outside his house; he gave us each a banana. He was asked if he was married; he said 'no', but he did have some children so no further questions were asked. We were then taken back to the meeting house and given some freshly cooked bread, fruit and lemon juice made from fresh lemons. The womenfolk serenaded us with local songs that were sung in harmony; this was so pleasant to listen to! Our goodbyes were said to the friendly people and our sarongs removed as we returned to the car, and back to the hotel. This was a fascinating experience.

The chief of the village

Top: self with chief's friend. Bottom: the chief of the village.

Top: Clive and I in the village. Bottom: two cattle we saw travelling in a pickup, which had been stopped by police.

Earlier in the day we had met up with a couple and their two children from Australia; they were interesting people as they originated from Leamington Spa in England. They had lived in Sydney for several years and were not interested in returning to England, as they had better prospects where they were. The hotel provided a babysitter at a cost to look after the children, so we had a relaxing evening with the couple.

In the garden back at the hotel the gardener made two hats for us out of leaves, as well as a handbag. We were not able to bring them back to England as it was plant material.

On one day we went on a tour to one of the islands, called Treasure Island! Here many water sports could be tried out. Clive enjoyed snorkelling in the sea, while I stayed relaxing on the beach in the shade admiring the various sports. A large lunch was prepared in the island kitchen; as it was so hot many drinks were served. The sea was a beautiful blue and it was calm for the crossing in both directions, which made it possible to see the fish under the glass-bottom boat. When we had returned to the hotel the evening was spent with the Australians.

Thursday, which was to be the last day! It was time to say goodbye to the Australians on their wedding anniversary. Staff came into the restaurant and sang several farewell songs, before we booked out of the hotel. We had a day to spend on another South Sea island; this was smaller than the one we had visited the previous day. Clive went snorkelling and unfortunately got into difficulties. Someone swimming close brought him to the shore. It was then I saw real problems; help came, in the person of the tutor for deep sea diving, and he gave Clive oxygen, and this brought him round. A speedboat was found and rushed us to the mainland where a car was waiting for us; it took us straight to a doctor, who sent Clive for an X-ray a few doors away. The doctor then sent him to the hospital at Lautoka. This was three quarters of an hour's drive from Nadi, as the local hospital was not suitable for tourists.

The tourist board were so helpful; they took me to the airport to explain the situation and to cancel our flights for that evening. The tourist manager booked a hotel in Lautoka, so as to be close to the hospital. I collected our luggage with the help of the tourist agent. Unfortunately his car broke down near Nadi, and after waiting for an unsuccessful repair he paid for a taxi to complete the trip back to Lautoka. I had to contact England to make sure someone would be around to look after our dogs.

The hospital was so basic it was a tale on its own! The state of the place was dreadful; walls and wards needed redecorating as they were minus a lot of paint, the bed in the emergency area had soiled sheets, curtains that were supposed to go round the bed were torn. When Clive was accepted into a ward, people were still all in their clothes, there were no blankets, sheets on the beds were also soiled, no pillows either. The food looked dreadful but none was offered to Clive. A patient in a bed behind, Joe, kindly gave him an apple, bananas and a drink, otherwise he would not have received anything.

We also met Joe's wife; her knowledge of the town and hospital was extremely helpful. I took her into town and purchased some things for Joe. We learnt he would not be able to work again; it sounded as if his health would not improve. He was a diabetic so later we sent some drugs for him. When we finally said goodbye Sai, his wife, burst into tears.

The hotel manager spoke to us after Clive came out of hospital; he tried to contact our insurance company in England. He spent two hours trying to organise everything for us.

The following evening we had a telephone call from the bank teller at the last hotel, where we had changed some travellers cheques. Later in the day she came with another woman and a boy friend. She declared that the wrong money had been given to us in exchange. We had our doubts as a gentleman had checked her money in the bank before she gave it to us. I think this was a scam; what was another woman who had nothing to do with the bank doing there? She had no identity and wanted £300! We truthfully said we did not have the money as Clive and I had to stay longer. She wanted us to pay when we got home. As far as we were concerned this was the end of the story, no money was sent.

The following morning a fax arrived regarding the insurance, asking if details were correct, so we had to start again!

We lived in luxury with milk and morning papers delivered every day we were there. Clive was not allowed to fly for at least a week. A pickpocket took $50 from Clive's back pocket, while we were in town.

The hotel had a guest laundry, which we made use of, having to stay longer. Clive slept most of the time. Saturday afternoon when work had finished three of the tourist staff came to our hotel to see Clive, bringing a large floral arrangement with exotic flowers including orchids, and a get well card. We felt so honoured to think they cared enough to travel, and remain with us for an hour before returning to Nadi, all without payment; such caring people we will never forget!

Having got used to the high temperature we walked into the town in the slow pace of 'Fiji time' but still had perspiration running down our faces, even when sitting down. It was good to come back to our room of 18°C!

Sunday we had a short walk to the town, but everywhere was closed; the Catholic church was full with people standing outside. The remainder of the day, Clive slept while I read a book.

The hotel overlooked the waterfront; when the tide was out the promenade was not particularly pleasant, as the smell from the beach was strong. It appeared that all the waste had drained into the sea.

Monday was the day we had to return to the hospital for Clive to have another X-ray, and Joe's wife Sai met us, taking us to the correct department; this saved wandering round trying to find the X-ray. Afterwards the 'all clear' was given to fly home. Sai needed to shop for Joe, so we took her by taxi and returned her to the hospital later.

In the afternoon we had an outing to Ba, the next town; the scenery was quite different, with undulating hills and pleasant views. It was worth the taxi fare!

The following day we booked a cruise for two hours on a sailing boat, but motors were used, not sails. We were greeted as we arrived on board by a team singing with guitar accompaniment, then served coffee and refreshments. In fun Clive was chosen as captain, and another man as his spokesman. The remainder of the day was spent on a South Sea island, where there were many water sports. Clive decided just to paddle; that was sufficient after the drama of the previous week. A tour in a glass-bottom boat took us out to see some of the fish and corals.

The glass was cracked in places and some water seeped into the boat, and had to be bailed out. I was quite relieved to reach dry land! A barbecue was held for lunch with fish, chicken and sausages and a choice of salads.

Returning to the mainland the crew sang many Fiji songs and all in harmony. This was a special harmony I have only heard on Fiji. They also demonstrated how to open a coconut in the native way. Back on the mainland a tourist board car met us and returned us to our hotel.

The last day here! Early in the morning we visited Joe and his wife in hospital, to say our goodbyes, then rested until it was time to go to the airport. I had arranged the new flights a day or two earlier. Everyone could not have been more helpful, with particular thanks to the tourist board and the manager of the hotel.

At the airport we had to be downgraded as there were no free seats to Los Angeles, but Clive was given five economy seats and behind him was an oxygen cylinder in case of emergency and I had two seats to myself. This was provided with a doctor's certificate.

In America we changed flights for Heathrow and were told we only had economy seats again, but just before going through the gates to get on the aircraft we were upgraded. On finding the seats we found we had been allocated first-class seats which could be made into beds. Consequently I had a very good sleep being able to travel in a prone position; so ended our eventful holiday! As previously planned we were met by taxi and driven home.

After all the excitement, it was good to be home!

Top: flowers and card on coming out of hospital. Bottom: view on the way up to the village.

Baltic Cruise
May 2012
(ten days)

After parking our car (free of charge), we rode on the shuttle service to the ship, the *MSC Opera*. We had to go through the ritual of customs, passports etc. and wait for some time before actually boarding; we heard afterwards inspectors had been on board ordering certain safety checks, e.g. releasing a life boat of their choice. Eventually we were allowed on board and made our way to our cabin on deck eight. We sailed at 5.30pm, an hour late. We walked round trying to find our way on the various main 11 decks.

Dinner was served at 6pm, a routine every night; we had been allocated the first sitting. Dress for several nights was casual, but at the two main gala dinners it was evening dress. After the first night we shared a table with the same couple. Each night there was a seven-course meal, although it was too much for me. I think Clive finished it twice!

After the first evening meal we booked the outings at ports where we could go ashore; there was a selection of two or three for each port. Two were free on this cruise; IJmuiden, Holland, was the first trip. This was a new port outside Amsterdam, and the first time the ship had moored there. IJmuiden comes from 'IJ', the name of a river, and 'muiden', meaning the mouth of the river. We docked at 9am, with 20 coaches waiting to take us, the passengers, on the three different tours arranged. We were told Amsterdam contained a population of 750,000 with over 600,000 cycles. The country was very flat, and almost all the ground was nine feet below sea level, but Rotterdam was 18 feet below! The city contained many canals and as housing had been limited many people now lived in boat houses on the canals.

To start the tour, having moved away from the dock area, we went through a large industrial estate, where many fish processing plants were preparing to export their goods, also a large steel works now bought by an Indian company.

Clive and I had decided to go on the countryside tour; this took us in a northerly direction on the polders. It could not have been a nicer time of year although it 'drizzled' with rain most of the way. It was spring, fresh green leaves on the trees, acres of bulb fields in bloom, and many narrow country lanes.

It was a treat to see many milking cows grazing outside. This particular area had many Friesian herds on very lush grass; some places also had sheep. The herds were a small size, perhaps a hundred! Clive noted there were no water troughs in the fields so supposed they drank from the dykes, although they had steep sides; he had visions of the animals falling in! There were also herds of goats, and cheese was made from their milk.

Four windmills at an open-air museum

One visit was to an open air museum which had four windmills; they were originally for pumping water from the dykes. A craft there was clog making, although they are mostly made for decoration now; we watched them being made. The original method took hours, but now German machines are used and a clog can be made in five minutes.

Clogs

A further stop was at the Edam cheese factory. The cheese maker showed us the various processes that went into making the cheeses; some were ready in months, and others took a year or two to mature sufficiently to eat. Many samples were available for us to taste, according to the age and type of milk used. There were samples of goats' and sheep's milk cheeses. We came away with a so-called 'young cheese' which had a good flavour. This tour was very interesting to me as I had only visited south of Amsterdam. This tour had taken five hours by the time we returned to the ship.

The following day was spent at sea, travelling to the north of Danmark and round southern Sweden into the Baltic. Along the coast northwards the sea was rough and I became seasick, so spent most of the day in bed. I did manage to get up and have my photo taken with the captain, although I missed out on the evening meal. We went to the theatre to see the 'illusion show', which Clive did not think much of as he knew how the tricks were done.

Tallinn square

Saturday we arrived in Tallinn, Estonia. Once again we had a coach take us into the town, stopping first at a hall where pop festivals were held. Later we came to the ruins of a convent and monastery, which had been burnt down in 1400 by the Danish.

There were 150 nuns and 90 monks living there at the time. We walked some distance and paid a visit to the Orthodox church which had beautiful decorations inside. Some streets were narrow, cobbled or with masses of steps. A large park we walked by, but it was very low level, whilst we walked up a steep hill; the trees had an almost black bark to the trunks. The central square was quite large with mostly restaurants and cafés. It was pleasant sitting outside enjoying our coffee, watching the world go by! Tallinn has a small population of 1.3 million, and only about 30% attend church.

Sunday was a day at sea but relatively calm; I joined a quiz with Clive but our results were not outstanding! The remainder of the day was spent relaxing until the evening meal. After this we went to see another show, a variety; nothing special and only three quarters of an hour, but like all entertainment on the cruise it was free.

St Petersburg, and again we arrived at a new dock where a considerable amount had been reclaimed. Another cruiser docked close to us just after we had arrived, called the *Northern Sun*. There were 32 coaches waiting for us, to take us to the city. We were all given stickers with our coach number on them, according to the tour we had chosen. We had a full day including a lunch provided. To me it seemed St Petersburg had been to war so many times, and gone through so many name changes, i.e. Leningrad, Stalingrad, and now back to St Petersburg. During the war in 1941 with Germany, there were over 1 million people killed, some German and some Russian, some even with starvation. There are many mass graves.

The famous fortress contained a beautiful church, where royalty have been buried. Although tombs were above ground they are buried six feet under the ground.

Repair work was being carried out, some people high in the roof, no safety protection while they were working. It was amazing! Women were replacing the gilt on pillars and ornate figures. St Peter's Church has the tallest spire, and could be seen all over the city.

It was a bright but chilly morning as we toured round in the coach. St Isaac's Cathedral had been repaired after the war. Many places were being torn down ready to be rebuilt in a newer style as many had been damaged by the 1941 siege. On my previous visit I could see damage to walls of the buildings from the war. From here we had an enjoyable meal at a hotel.

One place I was looking forward to visiting again was the hermitage. This time unfortunately the place was crowded, it rather spoilt the visit, but still I went round the museum that contained such delicate and beautiful works of art. It was still worth visiting for the second time. On the way back to the boat we stopped at the Church of Spilt Blood, so called after Alexander II was killed there and blood ran freely. I did not go in, but was told it cost several euros to enter. A market was on the opposite side of the road, selling many souvenirs, then back on board.

The next day a beautiful sunny day and we took a short trip into the city, but this was repeating many places visited the previous day, which I mentioned when questioned about the tours. The remainder of the day we spent on board.

Next morning was a travel quiz; once again we did nothing special. In the afternoon a talk was given on various scams.

The following day was a tour in Kobenhavn, which Clive went on. I had been there many times, having lived on the outskirts for a year. In the afternoon when Clive had returned a talk was given about the boat we were on: the *MSC Opera*.

MSC stands for Merchant Shipping Company. They have 470 cargo ships, 12 passenger ships. A container ship carries 1400 containers on one ship. The passenger ship carries approximately 2700 crew. The *Opera* was built in 2005; a new one was to be launched in a few days of this cruise, costing £600 million. All the company's passenger ships are named after Italian terms in music. The crew come from 39 different countries, all trades. A daily English lesson is given to improve their language. The ship takes 2.5 million litres of fuel, and we were told Sophia Loren launches all the company's ships.

The *Opera* is 753 feet long; it has heads for all the different departments on board. The braid on an employee's arm denotes which area or department they work in. The ships are made in parts and then put together as this allows for bad weather and helps to take the strain. There are two propellers at the stern and two thrusters at the bow; they all run by electricity. The ships go through a service every year and a refit every two years.

On the bridge is a cruise plan, containing charts for depth of water and wind speed, and a GPS backup; there is no ship's wheel, just a short driving stick. Safety fire people are always on board patrolling the ship; there are heavy fire doors in several places on all decks; as to sprinklers there are more than required. The ship has long-range communications and air conditioning.

Waste food is ground up and discharged into the sea. Water is desalinated for drinking, or fresh water can be collected at a port. Four thousand eggs a week are devoured; the ship has its own bakery catering for all the guests.

I spent half of Friday and all of Saturday in bed owing to seasickness, caused by the rough weather through the North Sea. As soon as we returned to the English Channel the sea became calm, and so did I! The ship was four hours late docking in Southampton. When we landed there was no passport control or customs to go through. We had the service shuttle to our car, and so the end of another holiday.

Opera and *Northern Sun*